INTERNATIONAL
GAMES

BUILDING SKILLS THROUGH MULTICULTURAL PLAY

GAYLE L. HOROWITZ

HUMAN KINETICS

Library of Congress Cataloging-in-Publication Data

Horowitz, Gayle L., 1971-
  International games : building skills through multicultural play /
Gayle L. Horowitz.
        p. cm.
  Includes bibliographical references.
  ISBN-13: 978-0-7360-7394-3 (soft cover)
  ISBN-10: 0-7360-7394-9 (soft cover)
1. Games. 2. Multicultural education--Activity programs. I. Title.
  GV1203.H626 2008
  790.1--dc22

                                        2008026084

ISBN-10: 0-7360-7394-9
ISBN-13: 978-0-7360-7394-3

The Web addresses cited in this text were current as of July 2008, unless otherwise noted.

Acquisitions Editor: Scott Wikgren
Developmental Editor: Melissa Feld
Assistant Editors: Anne Rumery and Rachel Brito
Copyeditor: Joy Wotherspoon
Proofreader: Coree Clark
Graphic Designer: Bob Reuther
Graphic Artist: Patrick Sandberg
Cover Designer: Keith Blomberg
Art Manager: Kelly Hendren
Associate Art Manager: Alan L. Wilborn
Illustrators: Jennifer Gibas and Keri Evans
Printer: United Graphics

Printed in the United States of America   10 9 8 7 6 5 4 3 2 1

Human Kinetics
Web site: www.HumanKinetics.com

United States: Human Kinetics
P.O. Box 5076
Champaign, IL 61825-5076
800-747-4457
e-mail: humank@hkusa.com

Canada: Human Kinetics
475 Devonshire Road Unit 100
Windsor, ON N8Y 2L5
800-465-7301 (in Canada only)
e-mail: info@hkcanada.com

Europe: Human Kinetics
107 Bradford Road
Stanningley
Leeds LS28 6AT, United Kingdom
+44 (0) 113 255 5665
e-mail: hk@hkeurope.com

Australia: Human Kinetics
57A Price Avenue
Lower Mitcham, South Australia 5062
08 8372 0999
e-mail: info@hkaustralia.com

New Zealand: Human Kinetics
Division of Sports Distributors NZ Ltd.
P.O. Box 300 226 Albany
North Shore City
Auckland
0064 9 448 1207
e-mail: info@humankinetics.co.nz

CONTENTS

GAME FINDER

CONTENTS BY REGION

Contents by Unit

(continued)

CONTENTS BY UNIT (CONTINUED)

PREFACE

We often forget that people from other cultures are similar to us. We live in different countries, wear different clothes, and eat different food. But throughout history, people in all parts of the world have had leisure time that they have used for sports and games. Games can show us the similarities between cultures and help us explore other traditions.

Ideally, this book will allow physical educators to align their classes with other disciplines. You can select games that match the subject areas of your players' other classes. The international sports and games found in this book help players ages 10 and older to both build their motor skills and realize just how small the world truly is.

This book can be used in two ways. You can either work progressively through the book by skill or teach the games by region. The game finder at the beginning of the book sorts this information for easy use of either option. Each unit in the book covers a basic skill and ends with a quiz on the material from the unit. The games are arranged progressively so that each activity builds upon skills taught in the preceding games. Most of the units introduce each sport or game with historical background and an equipment list. If you are able to align your classes with other disciplines, use the game finder that lists the sports and games by country. When teaching by regional method, check the games before and after your chosen game for skill progression and in soliciting responses from players in regard to game similarities.

Many of the sports and games found in this book require very little in the way of equipment, but some do require special equipment. In these cases, I have found that you can make equipment for a fraction of the cost of commercially-manufactured brands. I've included plans and instructions for making these items.

By starting this book, you have taken the first step in opening the eyes of your young players. Enjoy the trip.

PLAY	LANGUAGE
Juego	Spanish
Jeu	French
Spiel	German
Gioco	Italian
Jogo	Portuguese
Lek	Swedish
Spel (Stuk)	Dutch
Skuespill	Norwegian
Играть (Egrat) (short *a* sound)	Russian
Παιχνίδι (Pekso) (long *o* sound)	Greek

1

STRIKING

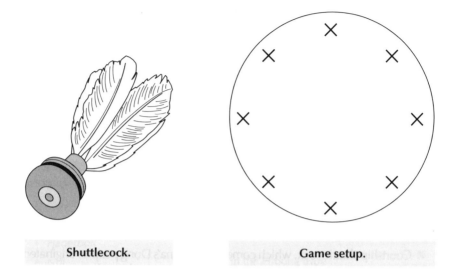

Shuttlecock.   Game setup.

Vᴀʀɪᴀᴛɪoɴs oғ Pʟᴀʏ

■ Players strike the shuttlecock to the person directly next to them. Continue around the circle in this manner.

■ Players may strike the shuttlecock around the circle in a random pattern and call out the name of the next player to hit the shuttlecock.

■ Using the random method, groups compete to see which one can keep the shuttlecock aloft the longest.

Sᴀғᴇᴛʏ

■ Groups should stand far enough apart to avoid contact.

■ Players in each circle should stand at least one arm's length apart from each other. They may put their arms out to the sides to measure the distance.

■ Players should not run outside the perimeter of the circle, but they may run toward the center or to the sides of the circle. If the shuttlecock travels outside the circle, players should let it drop. Any player who hits the shuttlecock out of the circle is penalized.

BATTLEDORE AND SHUTTLECOCK

Battledore and shuttlecock is a traditional keeping-up game from Native Americans. In a keeping-up game, players keep an object off the ground by striking it. The game is known as battledore and shuttlecock in the United States and Great Britain, and is known by many other names in different countries:

- Plumibal in Belgium, South Africa, and the Netherlands
- Le coquentin or le volant in France
- Federballspiel in Germany
- Hanetsuki in Japan
- Fjaderboll in Sweden
- Ndi in Thailand in the Hmong tribe

These variations of battledore and shuttlecock are similar to the games previously mentioned, but a paddle is used to strike the shuttlecock instead of a hand. The battledore may also be called either a washing beetle or a horn book. A washing beetle was a tool women used to beat the dirt out of their laundry. Some were as large as cricket bats and others were as small as table tennis paddles. The horn book, shaped like a table tennis paddle, was used for teaching children basic learning skills and was printed with letters, numbers, or prayers. Horn books are still used in some American churches today. Native Americans discovered the horn book through their interactions with European colonists and adopted it as a battledore for the game.

The game of badminton was derived from battledore and shuttlecock in the 1850s in England. Nobles played this variation of battledore and shuttlecock at the Duke of Beaufort's residence, which was called the Badminton House. The first rules for badminton were written in Poona, India, in 1873.

SIMILAR GAMES

Kalq is from Australia's Aboriginal people on the Cape York Peninsula. The men formed a circle and each player was armed with a small stick called a woomera. The first player tossed the large spear, or kalq, and players then used the woomera to deflect the kalq away from themselves and toward the next player. Young boys of the tribe also played this game but substituted a blunt-headed spear for the kalq, much like the other games of striking an object with a paddle-like object.

EQUIPMENT NEEDED

- Maps showing representations of North America from both the 16th century and the present time
- Modified shuttlecocks

- Table tennis paddles
- Floor marked with large circles. A circle for 5 players should be approximately 30 feet (9 m) in circumference. Add approximately 6 feet (2 m) to the circle for each additional player.

How to Play

1. Players form circles of 5 to 10 people.
2. The first person tosses the shuttlecock into the air and strikes it with the paddle.
3. Players continue to keep the shuttlecock aloft by striking it with their paddles and passing it to other players in a random pattern.
4. Players must hit the shuttlecock up, rather than laterally, so that the next player can easily hit it.
5. Players call out the letters of the alphabet or numbers in succession with each strike of the shuttlecock.

Variations of Play

- Players strike the shuttlecock to the person directly next to them. Continue around the circle in this manner.
- Players may strike the shuttlecock around the circle in a random pattern and call out the name of the next student to hit the shuttlecock.
- Have groups compete to see which one can keep the shuttlecock aloft the longest using the random method.

Safety

- Groups stand far enough apart to avoid contact.
- Players in each circle should stand at least one arm's length apart from each other. They may put their arms out to the sides to measure the distance.
- Players should not run outside the perimeter of the circle, but they may run toward the center or to the sides of the circle. If the shuttlecock travels outside the circle, players should let it drop. Any player who hits the shuttlecock out of the circle is penalized.

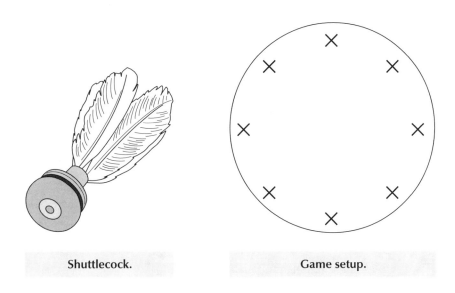

Shuttlecock.   Game setup.

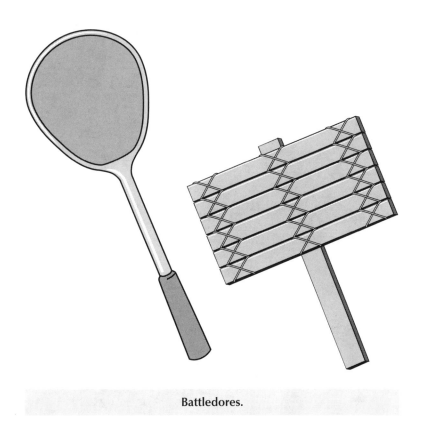

Battledores.

JEGI CHAGI

Jegi chagi is the modern version of a Korean game called chukguk. The game featured a handball-sized ball covered with leather and topped with a pheasant feather. The ball was filled with animal fur, straw, or the bladder of an ox or hog filled with air. The goal in jegi chagi is the same as the goal in chukguk: Players must keep the shuttlecock aloft using only their feet or legs. The game could be played alone or with a group.

The shuttlecock component of jegi chagi has also evolved. The large ball has been replaced by old coins with holes in the center. In some cases, the feather is inserted into paper that is wrapped around the coins. In other cases, fans of paper streamers resembling bird feathers project from the holes in the coins.

The game goes by other names in other countries:

- Chap-teh in Malaysia and Singapore
- Chiquia in Macau
- Da cau in Vietnam
- Jiann ji in China
- Kai mo in in Canton, China

EQUIPMENT NEEDED

- Map showing Korea
- Modified shuttlecocks
- Floor marked with large circles

SKILLS NEEDED

- Inner-foot kick
- Outer-foot kick
- Top-of-foot kick

Inner-foot kick.

Outer-foot kick.

Top-of-foot kick.

HOW TO PLAY

1. Players form circles of 5 to 10 people.
2. The first person tosses the shuttlecock into the air and kicks it.
3. Players continue to keep the shuttlecock aloft using various kicks and passing it to others in a random pattern.
4. Players must kick the shuttlecock up, rather than laterally, so that the next player can easily kick it.
5. Players call out letters of the alphabet or numbers in succession with each kick.

VARIATIONS OF PLAY

■ Players kick the shuttlecock to the person directly next to them. Continue around the circle in this manner.

■ Players kick the shuttlecock around the circle in a random pattern and call out the name of the next player to kick the shuttlecock.

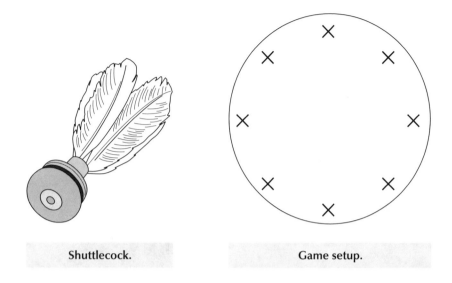

Shuttlecock.   Game setup.

▪ Using the random method, groups compete to see which one can keep the shuttlecock aloft the longest.

Safety

▪ Groups stand far enough apart to avoid contact.

▪ Players in each circle should stand at least one arm's length apart from each other. They may put their arms out to the side to measure the distance.

▪ Players should not run outside the perimeter of the circle, but they may run toward the center or to the sides of the circle. If the shuttlecock travels outside the circle, players should let it drop. Any player who kicks the shuttlecock outside the circle is penalized.

FOOTBAG AND WOGGABALIRI

Footbag is an ancient sport deeply rooted in North American and Asian cultures. Australia and Guatemala also have variations of the game. In Australia, the game is known as woggabaliri. It was a children's game played in New South Wales near the banks of the Bogan and Lachian rivers. The ball was made of opossum fur that was woven to create a ball approximately 5 centimeters in diameter. In Guatemala, footbag is played using a small, brightly colored woven ball filled with beans or seeds. In 1972, the American version known as Hacky Sack emerged when two athletes looking for a coordination-building game experimented with kicking a small beanbag around.

Regardless of the country, the rules of play are the same. Keep the beanbag or ball off the ground using only your feet or knees. The game can be played alone or with a group.

EQUIPMENT NEEDED

- Map showing Australia, Guatemala, and the United States
- Hacky Sacks, small beanbags, or Guatemalan footbags (woven cloth beanbags)
- Floor marked with large circles (have players stand in a circle with their arms outstretched to the sides)

SKILLS NEEDED

- Inner-foot kick
- Outer-foot kick
- Top-of-foot kick

HOW TO PLAY

1. Players form circles of 5 to 10 people per group.
2. The first person tosses the beanbag into the air and kicks it.
3. Players continue to keep the beanbag aloft using various kicks.

Inner-foot kick.

| Outer-foot kick. | Top-of-foot kick. |

4. Players must hit the beanbag up, rather than laterally, so that the next player can easily kick it.
5. Players call out the letters of the alphabet or numbers in succession with each kick.

VARIATIONS OF PLAY

■ Players kick the beanbag to the person directly next to them. Continue around the circle in this manner.

■ Players may kick the beanbag around the circle in a random pattern and call out the name of the next player to kick the beanbag.

■ Groups compete to see which one can keep the beanbag aloft the longest using the random method.

■ Players work individually, trying to keep the beanbag aloft as long as they can using a variety of kicks.

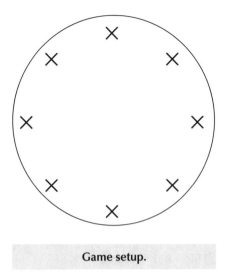

Game setup.

SAFETY

■ Groups stand far enough apart to avoid contact.

■ Players in each circle should stand at least one arm's length apart from each other. They may put their arms out to the sides to measure the distance.

■ Players should not run outside the perimeter of the circle, but they may run toward the center or to the sides of the circle.

SEPAK TAKRAW

The goal of the Thai game sepak takraw was similar to that of jegi chagi: to keep an object off the ground using the feet or legs. Villagers of all ages played the game to foster a sense of community, teamwork, and fun. Variations of the game were played in many Southeast Asian countries in the early 11th century:

▒ Sipa in the Philippines

▒ Sepakraga in Malaysia, Singapore, and Brunei

▒ Ching loong in Myanmar

▒ Rago in Indonesia

▒ Kator in Laos

Sepak takraw is a competitive game today. Over the years, players introduced alterations to rules and equipment to add to the excitement of the game. In the 19th century, players added a net, referees, and rules similar to modern volleyball. The net game consisted of three people on each side of the net working as a team. Players used their feet to introduce the ball into play in a manner similar to a volleyball serve. In 1984, a synthetic ball replaced the traditional rattan ball. This ensured uniformity of the balls for use in tournament play. In 1996, players began to stand in a circle and score points for each kick.

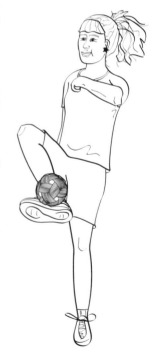

Inner-foot kick.

EQUIPMENT NEEDED

▒ World map (point out countries with variations of sepak takraw to show the widespread appeal of the game)

▒ Buka (woven rattan ball) or takraw balls

▒ Badminton nets set between 4 feet 8 inches (142 cm) and 4 feet 11 inches (150 cm) apart

▒ Floor marked with circles approximately 5 to 6 feet in circumference per student (e.g., 5 students would equal a circle with a circumference of 25 to 30 feet)

SKILLS NEEDED

▒ Inner-foot kick

▒ Outer-foot kick

▒ Top-of-foot kick

▒ Spike

▒ Serve

Outer-foot kick.

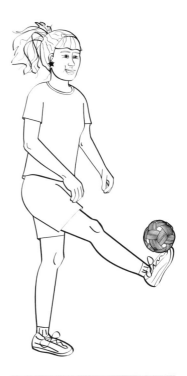

Top-of-foot kick.

Spike.

Serve.

SKILL BUILDING

1. Players form circles of 6 to 9 people.
2. The first person tosses the ball into the air and kicks it.
3. Players continue to keep the ball aloft by kicking it.
4. Players must kick the ball up, rather than laterally, so that the next player can easily kick it.
5. Players call out the letters of the alphabet or numbers in succession with each kick.
6. When players complete these skills, they learn the rules of volleyball and variations for sepak takraw.
7. Players practice kicking the ball over the net using various kicking skills (toe kick, inner- and outer-foot kicks, spike, and serve) in small groups or pairs.

How to Play

1. Play modified games without the spike in groups of 9. Players compete 3 on 3 with the third group officiating. Groups rotate the teams after approximately 15 points so that all have a chance to practice.
2. Players incorporate the spike as their skills advance.

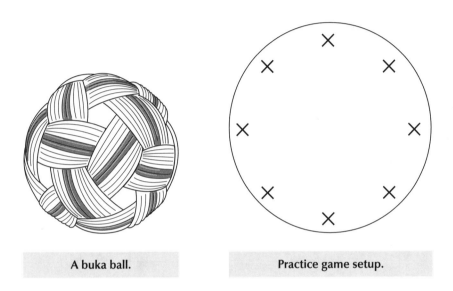

A buka ball.

Practice game setup.

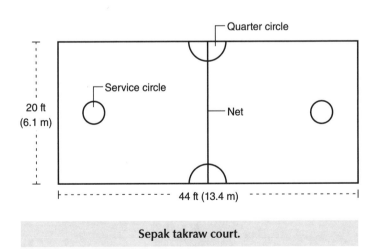

Sepak takraw court.

SAFETY

▦ Groups stand far enough apart to avoid contact.

▦ Players in each circle should stand at least one arm's length apart from each other. They may put their arms out to the sides to measure the distance.

▦ Players should not run outside the perimeter of the circle, but they may run toward the center of the circle or to the sides. If the ball travels outside the circle, players should let the ball drop. Any player who kicks the ball outside the circle is penalized.

VOLLEYBALL

In 1895, William G. Morgan, an instructor at the Holyoke YMCA in Massachusetts, created a game that combined the elements of basketball, baseball, tennis, and handball. His aim was to provide an activity for the businessmen attending YMCA classes that would have less physical contact than basketball.

In 1900, a special ball was designed for the sport. By 1916, the sport had a worldwide audience. In 1916, the offensive strategy known as the set and spike was developed in the Philippines. In 1928, it became apparent that due to the growing popularity of volleyball, tournaments and rules were needed. By 1951, volleyball was being played by more than 50 million people in over 60 countries. In 1964, volleyball was introduced as an Olympic sport.

In 1995, volleyball celebrated its 100th birthday. The sport has grown to include more than 46 million Americans and 800 million people worldwide who play volleyball at least once a week.

Name _____

INTERNATIONAL SPORTS AND GAMES

UNIT 1

1. What is a shuttlecock? Where does its name come from?

2. Name at least two similarities between peteca and battledore and shuttlecock.

3. Name at least two similarities among peteca, battledore and shuttlecock, and jegi chagi.

4. Name at least two similarities among jegi chagi, footbag, and sepak takraw.

5. Name at least two similarities between sepak takraw and volleyball.

MATCH THE GAME WITH THE COUNTRY

● ●

_____ Peteca   A. Colonial United States

_____ Battledore and shuttlecock   B. Korea

_____ Jegi chagi   C. Thailand

_____ Footbag   D. Brazil

_____ Sipa   E. Guatemala

_____ Sepak takraw   F. Philippines

From G. Horowitz, 2009, *International Games: Building Skills Through Multicultural Play* (Champaign, IL: Human Kinetics).

ACCURACY

KOOLCHEE

Koolchee is an Aboriginal form of bowling that was played in southern Australia. It was played with two teams; one offense and one defense. The offense's job was to knock over the pins at the center of the playing field by throwing balls at them. The defense's job was to block and redirect the offense's balls by hitting them with their own balls. The balls were made of easily-molded materials such as gypsum, sandstone, and mud. Koolchee could be played for hours on end.

EQUIPMENT NEEDED

- ▪ Indian clubs (long-necked bowling pin-shaped objects), plastic bowling pins, or one-liter soda bottles partially filled with sand
- ▪ Wiffle balls (softball size)
- ▪ Volleyball court, badminton court, or baseball field

HOW TO PLAY

1. Players form four teams of 5 to 10 people.
2. Two of the teams stand on opposite sides of the pins 60 to 90 feet (18 to 27 m) apart.
3. Each of the throwing teams gets an equal number of balls.
   a. One team acts as offense and tries to knock down the pins by rolling their balls at them.
   b. The other team acts as defense, and tries to block or redirect offensive attempts to knock down the pins by rolling or throwing their balls. Defense players may roll their balls along the ground, or throw the ball slightly above the ground at mid-calf height or lower.

4. The other two teams stand on opposite sidelines and maintain continuity of play by collecting and returning stray balls to the playing field.
5. Teams rotate and change roles when all pins are knocked down. This gives all teams a chance to play offense, defense, and sideline.

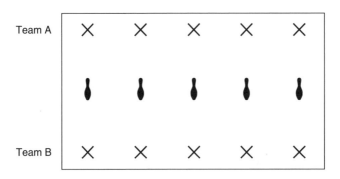

Game setup.

VARIATIONS OF PLAY

- Players line up pins near a wall and stand 20 to 40 feet (6 to 12 m) away. They try to knock down pins without interference. The winner is the team that knocks over the most pins.
- Players position the pins some distance away from the wall, then try to throw the ball so that it will strike the wall, ricochet off, and hit the pins on the return path.

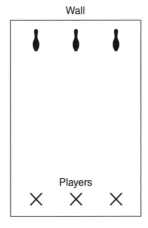

Game setup for play variation.

SAFETY

Players should throw the ball no higher than mid-calf level and may not throw it at people.

HORSESHOE PITCHING AND QUOITS

Horseshoe pitching and quoits are closely related and can be traced back to soldiers from the Roman Empire. During their free time, Roman soldiers entertained themselves by tossing metal rings or horseshoes at a stake in the ground. The game of quoits was played with a metal disk of the same name that had a hole in the middle. Soldiers tossed the quoits at a stake embedded in soft clay. Horseshoe pitching was played in the same manner, but players threw the metal shoes of horses or mules.

During the 14th century, English rulers felt the game distracted the soldiers from their military training and outlawed the game in 1388. By the 16th century, English peasants picked up the game. Immigrants who moved to North America continued playing it there. North American soldiers, like the Roman soldiers, found the game of horseshoe pitching to be good wartime recreation. When the soldiers returned to their homes after the Revolutionary War, they brought the game to communities across the United States and Canada.

EQUIPMENT NEEDED

▪ Stakes for outdoor play or stands with posts for indoor play

▪ Rings or rubber horseshoes

▪ Space for an alley 50 feet long (15 m) and 10 feet wide (3 m)

HOW TO PLAY

1. Players begin with a coin toss to determine who will throw first.

2. The game is divided into innings of two tosses per side.

3. Each team takes turns tossing both of the horseshoes or rings. The pitchers cannot step over the foul line drawn 3 feet (1 m) in front of the stake.

4. After completing the inning, the pitchers walk to the stake where the horseshoes or rings were tossed. They determine the number of points by counting the number of throws each team landed on the stake. The process is repeated in the opposite direction with a new team member from each side.

5. An official tournament is considered completed after players score 40 points or complete a total of 40 tosses over 20 innings. Recreational play is played to 15 to 21 total points. Players break ties with an additional two-inning match.

SCORING

▪ A horseshoe or ring that lands around the stake is called a ringer and is worth 3 points.

▪ If no player scores a ringer, the horseshoe or ring that is closest to the post is awarded 1 point.

ETIQUETTE

▪ Players should not talk or make sounds while their opponents toss.

▪ Participants may not go to the other stake or remove horseshoes or rings before the completion of an inning.

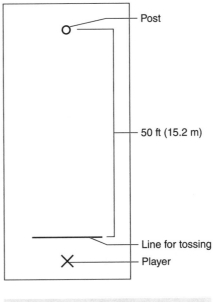

Game setup.

VARIATION OF PLAY

Use a five-post variation with points clearly marked.

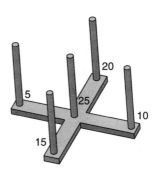

Five-post variation.

SAFETY

Place the posts so that the pitcher is throwing toward the wall at all times.

WEME

The Walbiri people of central Australia played a stone bowling game called weme. The name comes from the Eastern Arrernte language and means "throwing something at something else." A player throws the first stone. Once it lands, this stone becomes the target for the second player. Players take turns aiming at their opponent's stones.

EQUIPMENT NEEDED

- Set of 3 to 5 small balls for each pair of players
- Floor tape

HOW TO PLAY

1. Participants divide into pairs and toss a coin to determine who begins the game.
2. The first player stands behind a line and attempts to roll the ball toward another line 30 feet (9 m) away. The goal is to roll the ball within the bounds of the lines.
3. If the ball does not pass the far line, it is considered a fair ball. If the ball passes the line, the opponent scores a point.
4. If the ball is a fair ball, the second player rolls with the intent to strike the opponent's ball. A successful hit scores a point.
5. The players take turns rolling the balls.
6. The game is played until one of the players scores 11 points.

VARIATIONS OF PLAY

- For large groups: When all the pairs have completed their matches, the first thrower moves down the line to the right. This pattern continues until all of the throwers reach the end of the line. The remaining thrower who was unable to rotate goes to the line with the second throwers, and all the remaining players rotate to the left. The remaining second thrower moves into the first line (see pattern below).

$$B \leftarrow B \leftarrow B \leftarrow B \leftarrow B \leftarrow B$$
$$\downarrow \qquad\qquad\qquad\qquad\qquad \uparrow$$
$$A \rightarrow A \rightarrow A \rightarrow A \rightarrow A \rightarrow A$$

■ Place 3 balls in a circle between 2 players. Each player stands 30 feet (9 m) away from the circle and takes turns throwing at the balls in the center. Their aim is to strike the balls in the center and knock them out of the circle. Players score a point for each ball that is knocked out. When one person reaches 11 points, players rotate as in the preceding game.

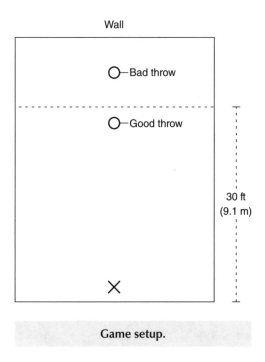

Game setup.

BOCCE

Bocce is a game that has been played for thousands of years. Egyptian drawings dating back to 5000 BC show people playing a form of bocce. In 800 BC, the game moved from Egypt to Greece and then moved from Greece to the Roman Empire. Bocce then moved into Italy, where the sport gained its popularity. Like horseshoes, quoit, and other games from the Middle Ages, bocce was banned by military leaders because they thought the game distracted the soldiers. The penalties for playing the game ranged from fines to prison. The Catholic Church also banned bocce because the religious leaders believed the game led to gambling.

Bocce is a combination of horseshoes, bowling, shuffleboard, and billiards. Bocce can be played on almost any surface, and requires both strategy and accuracy. It is now played worldwide. In France it is known as *boules* and in England it is known as *lawn bowls*.

SIMILAR GAMES

Petanque from France is similar to bocce. The game's origin is less demanding; a game from southern France called *Jeu Provencal*. The name *petanque* comes from the Old French *pieds tanques* meaning fixed feet because the game is played by keeping both feet together. Players throw metal balls as close as possible to a small wooden ball. In bocce, players also attempt to get their balls as close as possible to a small target ball, but they roll the balls instead of throwing them.

EQUIPMENT NEEDED

For each group of four:

- 1 tennis ball or handball
- 8 softballs or Wiffle balls in two different colors

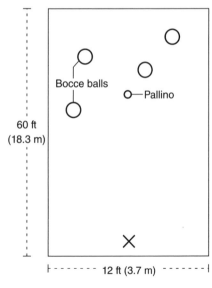

Game setup.

HOW TO PLAY

1. Divide the players into pairs. Each team of two will play another team of two.

2. Players flip a coin to determine the order of play. The winner of the coin toss also gets first choice of ball color.

3. The first player tosses the pallino (the handball or tennis ball) toward the end of the alley.

4. This player also gets to throw the first ball (the softball). Balls may be thrown or rolled in one of three ways:

   a. Players aim directly at the pallino in an attempt to get their ball as close as possible. This throw is called a *punto*. If the ball lands touching the pallino, it is called a *baci* (kiss).

   b. Players aim directly at another player's ball in an attempt to move it out of the way. This throw is called a *raffa*.

   c. Players throw the ball in the air to move another ball out of the way.

5. At the end of each round, one point is given for each ball that is closer to the pallino than the other team's balls.

6. All throws must be made from behind the line.

SAFETY

For increased safety, use beanbags or fabric balls to play petanque.

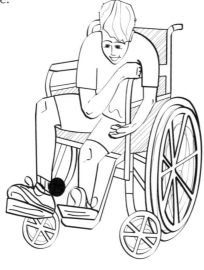

Playing bocce.

'ULU MAIKA

'Ulu maika is a game that was developed shortly after Hawaii was discovered around 450 AD. Sports in Hawaii were used as training for war. These games focused on endurance, strength, skill, and accuracy. 'Ulu maika developed both strength and accuracy. Players rolled a stone disk to a point 30 feet (9 m) away and attempted to get the disk between two sticks lying 6 inches (15 cm) apart.

EQUIPMENT NEEDED

■ 2 cones

■ 2 disks for every 6 to 10 players made from either wood or foam. Disks should be 8 to 12 inches (20 to 30 cm) in diameter.

■ An area approximately 60 feet (18 m) long

HOW TO PLAY

1. The playing area is set up with 2 cones approximately 6 inches (15 cm) apart in the center and 2 lines marked 30 feet (9 m) away from the cones.

2. Participants divide into teams of 3 to 5 players.

3. Each team stands on opposite sides behind the lines and receives a disk.

4. Teams take turns trying to roll the disk between the cones. They receive 1 point for each successful roll. The team with the most points wins.

5. Each player should be allowed to roll the disk at least once.

SAFETY

Wooden disks should be filed down well or wrapped with electrical tape to prevent splinters.

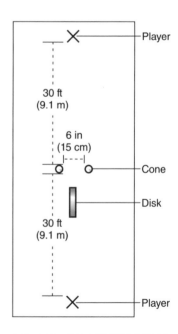

Game setup.

Kubb

The history of kubb (pronounced *koob*) spans more than 1000 years. Kubb started when Viking children created a game with the remnants of chopped wood. The word *kubb* comes from the Swedish word *kubben,* which means block of wood or branch.

Kubb uses pieces of wooden blocks and combines the strategies of chess and the French game of boules. The object is to use throwing sticks, or batons, to knock over all the kubbs of the opposing teams so players have a clear shot to knock over the king.

Equipment Needed

For each group:

- 10 kubbs, 6 inches (15 cm) high and 3 inches (8 cm) wide
- 1 king, 12 inches (30 cm) high and 4 inches (10 cm) wide
- 6 batons, 12 inches (30 cm) high and 2 inches (5 cm) wide
- 4 cones to mark off the field

How to Play

1. Players divide into teams of at least 6 people. (If necessary, the game may be played with less than 6 people.)
2. A space of 20 feet (6 m) by 13 feet (4 m) is marked as the playing field with 5 kubbs on one baseline (short side) and 5 kubbs on the opposite baseline (long side). The king is positioned in the center of the playing field.
3. Team 1 begins by using the throwing sticks to knock over their opponents' kubbs. Players should flip the throwing sticks end-over-end, and may not use direct throws or helicopter throws.
4. Team 2 has two attempts to take back their kubbs. Any kubbs knocked over in an opponent's half of the field are called *field kubbs.* The field kubbs are placed upright where they landed. If the throws are unsuccessful, team 1 may place these field kubbs anywhere on their half of the field. Field kubbs must be positioned at least one throwing stick's distance away from the king and other kubbs.
5. Team 2 now has the opportunity to knock over the other team's kubbs. They must knock over the field kubbs from the first round before they can aim for kubbs on the baseline.
6. Team 1 must give any fallen kubbs to team 2. Any field kubbs that are knocked over are removed from play.

7. The game continues in this manner until one team knocks over all of the opposing team's kubbs. Once all the kubbs have been knocked over, teams can aim for the king.

a. Players may not hit the king until all of the opponent's kubbs have been knocked down. Any player who strikes the king early surrenders the remainder of their team's turn, and the king is returned to an upright position.

b. Players must throw from behind the baseline.

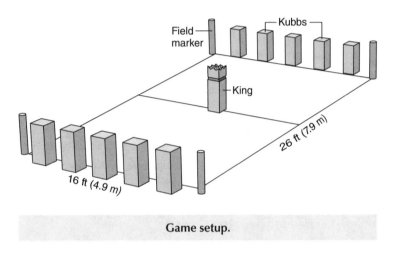

Game setup.

SAFETY

Players may construct throwing sticks from foam to reduce the risk of injury.

BOWLING

Bowling is popular all around the world, and many different countries claim a part in the game's history. In the 1930s, anthropologists in Egypt found ancient objects that looked like primitive bowling equipment in a child's grave. These artifacts dated back to 3200 BC. German historians claim bowling originated in Germany around 300 AD. The first written mention of bowling is in British documents from the late 1300s that list bowling as an illegal activity that distracted from military exercises. King Henry VIII later reinstated bowling as an appropriate pastime.

Bowling came to the New World with the English, Dutch, and German settlers. In 1895, the first standardized set of rules was created in New York City, where the American Bowling Congress was founded, and national competitions began shortly after. The Women's International Congress was founded in 1917, which later evolved into the Women's National Bowling Association.

Bowling continued to grow in popularity as the years progressed. The bowling ball that we know today was introduced in 1914 and the commercial pin setting machine was introduced in 1952. Bowling first appeared on television in the 1950s; some game shows featured bowling and the Pro Bowlers tour was first broadcast in 1961. The addition of ball and shoe rentals made bowling available to all who wanted to play.

INTERNATIONAL SPORTS AND GAMES

UNIT 2

1. How are weme, bocce, and petanque similar?

2. How were horseshoe pitching, quoits, and bocce seen by the government? What penalties were imposed on players?

3. How are bocce and petanque similar? How are they different?

4. How were traditional Hawaiian games used?

5. How is the game of kubb similar to the game of chess?

MATCH THE GAME WITH THE COUNTRY

. . . .

_____ Kubb		A. Roman empire
_____ Koolchee		B. Hawaii
_____ Quoits		C. Sweden
_____ Bocce		D. Australia
_____ 'Ulu maika		E. France
_____ Petanque		F. Italy

RELAY
RACES

GAME	COUNTRY	PAGE
▦ Egg and spoon race	Colonial United States	36
▦ Potato sack race	Colonial United States	38
▦ Chopstick challenge	China	40
▦ Tarnambi	Australia	42
▦ Mukade kyoso	Japan	44

Before there were video games and satellite dishes, children played outside and created games from their imaginations. When children invented games, nothing was off limits. They used sticks as tools to draw lines in the dirt, coins as targets, and discarded items as toys. This section contains races that incorporate this childlike creativity. In addition to running skills, these races include balance, agility, and cooperation. They were run for both fun and competition.

EGG AND SPOON RACE

The egg and spoon race is a popular game at modern field days and picnics. The game originated in the Colonial United States. Traditionally, each player is given a standard wooden kitchen spoon and an egg. The object of the game is to move quickly to a finishing point while balancing the egg on the spoon. The spoon can be held in a variety of ways. Some players hold the spoon in one hand at arm's length, and others hold it between their teeth while keeping their hands behind their backs. If the egg is real, it makes quite a mess when it falls. When the game spread to schools, players started substituting a wooden or rubber egg to eliminate mess. This change made the egg and spoon race even more popular.

EQUIPMENT NEEDED

For each group:

- ▦ 1 cone
- ▦ 1 egg or small ball
- ▦ 1 wooden spoon

HOW TO PLAY

1. The playing area is set up with a starting line marked on the floor and a cone placed at a distance designating the point where players turn around. This distance varies based on the age and number of participants.

2. Players divide into teams of equal number. Team members line up behind the starting line.

3. The first person in line on each team receives one egg and one spoon.

4. Each participant must travel holding the egg on the spoon away from the body.

5. When players reach the cone, they switch the egg and spoon to the other hand, run around the cone, and return to the starting line.

6. When players return to the starting area, they pass the spoon to the next person in line. This process continues until all players have competed.

7. The first team to send all its members through the course is the winner.

Pᴏᴛᴀᴛᴏ Sᴀᴄᴋ Rᴀᴄᴇ

The potato sack race is another outdoor game that is popular today. It came from the Colonial United States. Traditionally, each player competes standing inside a potato sack. The object of the game is to jump as quickly as possible to a finishing point while staying inside the sack. When markets stopped selling potatoes in traditional sacks, sporting goods companies started making sacks for racing from burlap or nylon.

Eᴏᴜɪᴘᴍᴇɴᴛ Nᴇᴇᴅᴇᴅ

For each group:

- 2 potato sacks
- 1 cone

Hᴏᴡ ᴛᴏ Pʟᴀʏ

1. The playing area is set up with a starting line marked on the floor and a cone placed at a distance designating the point where players turn around. This distance varies based on the age and number of participants.
2. Players divide into teams of equal number. Team members line up behind the starting line.
3. The first two players in each line receive a potato sack and step inside to begin.
4. On the start signal, the players first in line hop to the cone, go around it, and return to the starting line.
5. Once the first player crosses the starting line, the second teammate begins the relay.
6. The player who has just returned steps out of the sack and hands it to the next teammate in line. Players step into sacks immediately when they receive them so they are ready to begin hopping as soon as the current racer returns.
7. This process continues until all players have competed.
8. The first team to send all its members through the course is the winner.

Vᴀʀɪᴀᴛɪᴏɴs ᴏғ Pʟᴀʏ

- Each team receives only one sack, so players cannot get into the sacks ahead of time. After completing their leg of the race, players must get out of the sack and hand it off to their teammates. Once the new players receive the hand-off, they must step completely into the sack before they resume the race.

■ Teams divide into two groups; one half of the team stands behind the original starting line and the other half stands behind the cone. Players race back and forth between the two markers and pass off the bags as in the preceding example.

CHOPSTICK CHALLENGE

The chopstick challenge is similar to the egg and spoon race except when played in China the equipment changed. In this relay, there is a bowl of cotton balls in front of each team instead of eggs. Each player picks up one of the cotton balls with the chopsticks, carries it using the chopsticks to a second bowl a set distance away, runs back to the starting line, and passes the chopsticks to the next player.

EQUIPMENT NEEDED

For each group:

- 2 small bowls
- 1 pair of chopsticks
- Bowl of cotton balls (one ball for each member of the team)

HOW TO PLAY

1. The playing area is set up with a starting line marked on the floor and an empty bowl placed at a distance designating the point where players turn around. This distance varies based on the age and number of participants.
2. Players divide into teams of equal number and line up behind the starting line.
3. Each team receives a bowl filled with cotton balls and places it in front of the starting line. There should be one cotton ball in the bowl for each teammate.
4. The first player on each team receives a pair of chopsticks.
5. Using the chopsticks, the first person must carry a cotton ball to the empty bowl and deposit it there, run back to the starting line, and pass off the chopsticks to the next player in line.
6. Player 2 repeats this process. This pattern continues until all the players have competed and all the cotton balls have been transferred to the second bowl.
7. The first team to send all its members through the course and transfer all the cotton balls is the winner.

VARIATIONS OF PLAY

Each player must transfer all the cotton balls, one at a time, from one bowl to the other using the chopsticks. Once the initial players have transferred all the cotton balls to the far bowl, they return to the starting line and hand off the chopsticks to their teammates. This player runs to the second bowl and begins to return all the cotton balls to the original bowl. When all cotton balls are returned to the original bowl, the chopsticks are handed off to the next player. This pattern continues until all players have competed. The first team to send all its members through the course is the winner.

TARNAMBI

Tarnambi comes from the Australian island of Bathurst. In the earlier version of the game, school children collected the seed heads of the grass and brought them to the beach. They tossed the seeds up in the air where the wind caught them, then chased after them and tried to catch them. Tarnambi is played using balls instead of grass. One player rolls a ball while another tries to retrieve and return it faster than their opponents.

EQUIPMENT NEEDED

For each group:

- 1 cone
- 1 tennis ball

HOW TO PLAY

1. The playing area is set up with a starting line marked on the floor and an end line marked 40 to 60 feet (12 to 18 m) away.
2. Divide the players into teams of equal numbers. All players line up behind the starting line.
3. One member of the team rolls a tennis ball towards the end line, and then moves to the back of the line.
4. Once the ball crosses the end line, the second player runs to retrieve the ball, returns it to the next player as quickly as possible, then moves to the back of the line. The player at the head of the line rolls the ball.
5. This process continues until all teammates have had a chance to either throw or retrieve. The team that returns all the thrown balls first is declared the winner.

Mᴜᴋᴀᴅᴇ Kʏᴏsᴏ

October 10th is a national holiday in Japan in which schools practice a sports day called an *undokai*. The undokai includes both traditional sports and games similar to American field day activities like relay races, three-legged races, and tug-of-war. One of the activities played during an undokai is *mukade kyoso*. *Mukade* is the Japanese word for centipede and *kyoso* means to compete.

Eǫᴜɪᴘᴍᴇɴᴛ Nᴇᴇᴅᴇᴅ

- ▦ Cloth ties or Velcro straps
- ▦ Tape or cones to mark start and finish lines
- ▦ Map showing Japan

Hᴏᴡ ᴛᴏ Pʟᴀʏ

1. The playing area is set up with a starting line marked on the floor or ground and a finish line marked some distance away. The distance apart should be determined based on age of the players and the size of the teams.

2. Players divide into teams of 6 to 8 people.

3. Each team forms a line standing side by side. Arrange the players on each line so that every other player faces in one direction and the other players face in the other direction.

4. The players attach their legs to those of their neighbors using the cloth or Velcro straps. This tying configuration is similar to the one used for a three-legged race.

5. The object of the game is to be the first team to walk as a unit past the finish line. The winning team will be one that can work cooperatively as well as quickly.

INTERNATIONAL SPORTS AND GAMES

UNIT 3

1. Name at least two similarities between the egg and spoon race and the chopstick challenge.

2. What is the most important skill needed for mukade kyoso?

3. What do the egg and spoon race, the potato sack race, and the chopstick challenge have in common?

4. What is the most important part of all of the relay races?

MATCH THE GAME WITH THE COUNTRY

_____ Mukade kyoso   A. Colonial United States

_____ Potato sack race   B. Japan

_____ Egg and spoon race   C. Colonial United States

_____ Chopstick challenge   D. Australia

_____ Tarnambi   E. China

HOPSCOTCH

HOPSCOTCH

Hopscotch is a game played by hopping or jumping through a series of boxes marked on the ground. The name hopscotch comes from the words *hop* and *escocher*. *Escocher* is a old French word meaning to cut. Originally, squares were scored into the ground to create the pattern.

Hopscotch can be traced back to the time of the Roman Empire, which encompassed most of modern Europe. Hopscotch patterns have been found among the ancient Roman ruins. The original courts were over 100 feet (30 m) long and were used by the military for training. The soldiers wore full gear and ran through the course in a manner similar to the training methods of American football teams. When Roman children began to play, they shortened the length of the court, and later players in other countries added jumps, hops, and other variations.

EQUIPMENT NEEDED

- ▩ World map showing all the countries outlined in this unit
- ▩ Small beanbags for tossing
- ▩ Commercial grade carpeting and paint, secure canvas tarps and paint, chalk, or floor tape

ESCARGOT (SNAIL) OR LA MARELLE RONDE

This French version of the game has two names: *escargot*, which means snail, and *la marelle ronde*, which means round hopscotch.

HOW TO PLAY

1. The player's goal each turn is to hop on one foot through the entire pattern without hopping on any lines.

2. Players are allowed only one hop per square and may rest only after box 17 (rest square).

3. When they reach the end of the pattern, players repeat the pattern in reverse (boxes 17 through 1).

4. After completing the pattern, players choose a square as their *house*, and mark it with their names or initials.

5. No one can hop in a box that has been claimed except for the person who has claimed it.

6. Each player repeats this sequence until so many squares have been filled that it is impossible to jump to an available square.

7. The player with the most claimed squares wins.

PLAYERS LOSE A TURN IF THEY JUMP ON THE LINES.

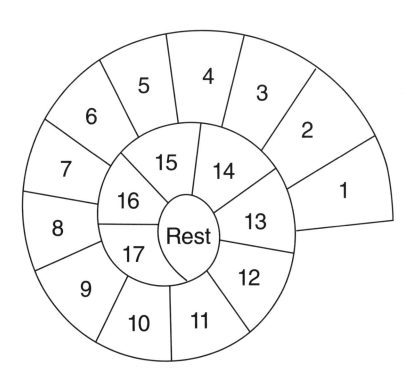

POTSY

Potsy is an American version of hopscotch played in Brooklyn, New York.

HOW TO PLAY

1. Players alternate turns completing the following process.
2. Player 1 tosses the marker into box 1. Players must not jump in any box containing a marker.
3. The player moves though the pattern, skipping box 1 and the marker, hopping in single boxes and jumping with both feet in paired boxes.
4. Upon reaching the end of the pattern, player 1 jumps and turns to face the opposite direction.
5. The player returns to the box just prior to the one with the marker in it.
6. The player picks up the marker, completes the pattern by continuing to the end, and hops out.
7. Player 2 now tosses a marker into box 1 and proceeds with the pattern. Once all players have completed the first round, they throw their markers into box 2. On the third round, players aim their markers at box 3, and so on. The game is over when each player has successfully thrown the marker into each box (1 through 8) and has jumped through the pattern accordingly.

Players lose a turn if they jump on the lines or toss the marker into the wrong box.

7	8

| 6 | |

4	5

| 3 | |

1	2

Il Gioco del Mondo

Il gioco del mondo is from Italy and uses both oval and square spaces.

How to Play

1. Players stand approximately 3 feet (1 m) from the start of the board and toss a marker into space 1.

2. They move through the pattern one player at a time, hopping on the single spaces, jumping in the paired spaces, and avoiding the ovals with no numbers until they reach the rest space.

3. In the rest space, players hop and turn to face the other direction.

4. They continue hopping back through the pattern, stopping one space before the one with the stone (for example, players stop in space 2 if the stone is in space 1). They should not let the other foot touch the ground as they bend and pick up the stone.

5. This process continues until one player has thrown the marker successfully in spaces 1 through 7.

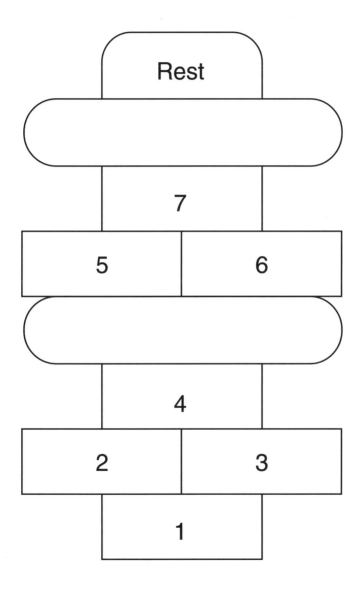

Rest

7

5 6

4

2 3

1

PELE

Pele comes from Aruba. It is also known as *Klassa* in Poland and *Jumby* in Trinidad and Tobago.

HOW TO PLAY

1. Players alternate turns completing the following process.
2. Player 1 tosses the marker into box 1. Players must not jump in any box containing a marker.
3. The player moves through the pattern, skipping box 1 and the marker, hopping in single boxes and jumping with both feet in paired boxes.
4. Upon reaching the end of the pattern, player 1 jumps and turns to face the opposite direction.
5. The player returns to the box just prior to the one with the marker in it.
6. The player picks up the marker, completes the pattern by continuing to the end, and hops out.
7. Player 2 now tosses a marker into box 1 and proceeds with the pattern. Once all players have completed the first round, they throw their markers into box 2. On the third round, players aim their markers at box 3, and so on.
8. The game is over when each player has successfully thrown the marker into each box (1 through 7) and has jumped through the pattern accordingly.

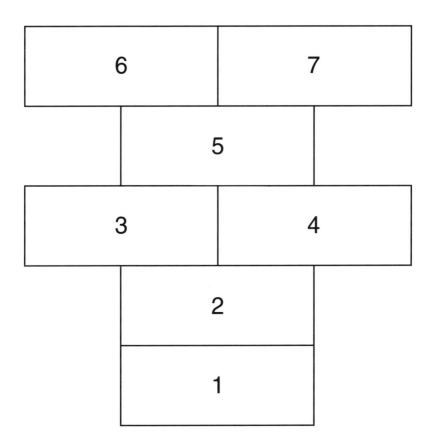

TEMPLEHUPFEN

Templehupfen is the German version of hopscotch.

HOW TO PLAY

1. Players stand with their back to the game area.
2. They toss the markers over their shoulders.
3. The box in which the stone lands is called that player's *house*, and is marked with the player's name.
4. Players hop through the entire grid, forward and back, without missing a box or stepping on a line.
5. If the players are successful, they get to keep ownership of their houses.
6. No player may step in another player's house.
7. The game continues until the grid is so full of claimed houses that it is not possible for players to make successful jumps.

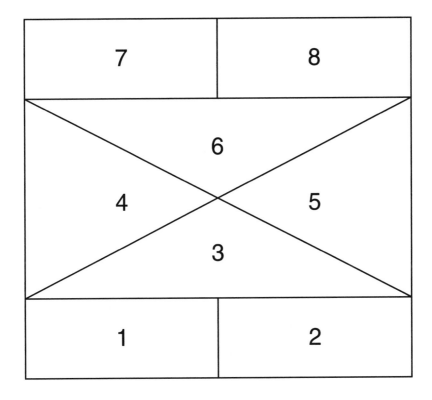

RAYUELA

Rayuela comes from Colombia.

HOW TO PLAY

1. Players alternate turns completing the following process.
2. Player 1 tosses the marker into box 1. Players must not jump in any box containing a marker.
3. The player moves through the pattern, skipping box 1 and the marker, hopping in single boxes and jumping with both feet in paired boxes.
4. Upon reaching the end of the pattern, player 1 jumps and turns to face the opposite direction.
5. The player returns to the box just prior to the one with the marker in it.
6. The player picks up the marker, completes the pattern by continuing to the end, and hops out.
7. Player 2 now tosses a marker into box 1 and proceeds with the pattern. Once all players have completed the first round, they throw their markers into box 2. On the third round, players aim their markers at box 3, and so on.
8. The game is over when each player has successfully thrown the marker into each box (1 through 8) and has jumped through the pattern accordingly.

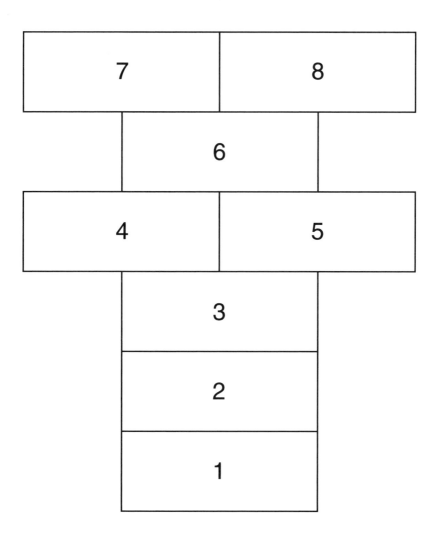

SCOTCH-HOPPERS

Scotch-hoppers comes from England.

HOW TO PLAY

1. Players toss the marker into box 1.
2. They move through the puzzle, hopping in each box individually (there are no paired box jumps).
3. When players reach the end, they jump and turn to face the opposite direction.
4. They return to the box before the one with the marker in it.
5. With their free foot, they kick the marker out of the pattern and over the baseline.
6. Players continue this process for each box (1 through 10) and jump out of the pattern when they reach the end.

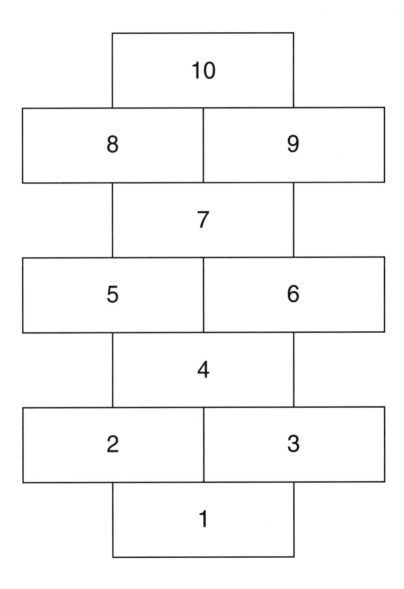

UGRÓISKOLA

Ugróiskola comes from Hungary.

HOW TO PLAY

1. Players toss the marker into box 1.
2. They hop into single boxes and jump into paired boxes. The box marked with an X is designated as *hell* and must be avoided.
3. When players reach the end, they jump and turn to face the opposite direction.
4. Players return to the box preceding the one with the marker in it.
5. They pick up the marker and throw it out of the pattern.
6. Players continue this process for each box (1 through 5) and jump out of the pattern when they reach the end.

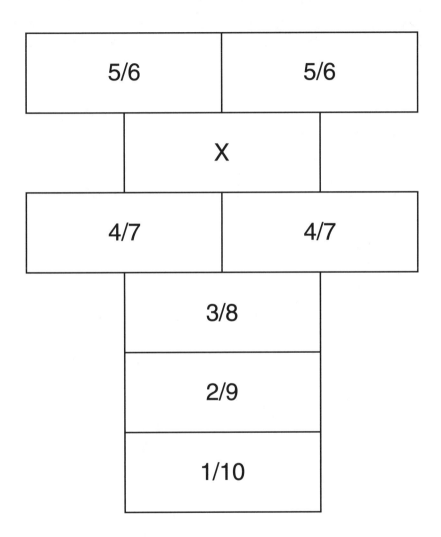

5/6	5/6

X

4/7	4/7

3/8

2/9

1/10

INTERNATIONAL SPORTS AND GAMES

UNIT 4

1. Where did the idea of hopscotch come from?

2. What country does the round hopscotch game come from? What is it called? Why?

3. In Alaskan hopscotch, what is the marker that is tossed called?

4. What is the one rule that all of the hopscotch games have in common?

5. What are the main skills needed for all the hopscotch games?

MATCH THE GAME WITH THE COUNTRY

_____ Potsy   A. Germany

_____ Klassa   B. Aruba

_____ Rayuela   C. England

_____ Pele   D. Poland

_____ Il gioco del mondo   E. United States

_____ Scotch-hoppers   F. Italy

_____ Templehupfen   G. Colombia

From G. Horowitz, 2009, *International Games: Building Skills Through Multicultural Play* (Champaign, IL: Human Kinetics).

RHYTHM

CHINESE JUMP ROPE

Chinese jump rope combines the skills of hopscotch with some of the patterns from the hand-and-string game cat's cradle. The game began in 7th-century China. In the 1960s, children in the Western hemisphere adapted the game. German-speaking children call Chinese jump rope *gummitwist* and British children call it *elastics*.

The game is typically played in a group of at least 3 players with a rope approximately 16 feet (5 m) in length tied into a circle. Traditional Chinese jump ropes are strings of rubber bands tied together, but today many varieties of commercial rope exist. Two players face each other standing 9 feet (3 m) apart, and position the rope around their ankles so that it is taut. The third player stands between the two sides of the rope and tries to perform a designated series of moves without making an error or pausing. If the jumping player is successful, the players holding the rope increase the height by moving the rope up their legs to the mid-calf area or knee. The jumping player tries to complete the pattern again at the new height.

EQUIPMENT NEEDED

▨ 6 feet (2 m) minimum of elastic rope for each group

▨ Map showing China

HOW TO PLAY

1. Players divide into groups of a minimum of 3 players.

2. The playing area is set up with postings of various patterns (see figures, pages 69–73). The Xs represent the holders' feet and the remaining shape is the rope configuration.

3. After all patterns have been completed, players may create their own patterns incorporating the steps they've learned.

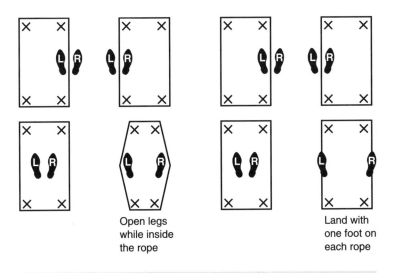

Open legs
while inside
the rope

Land with
one foot on
each rope

Pattern 1: Americans.

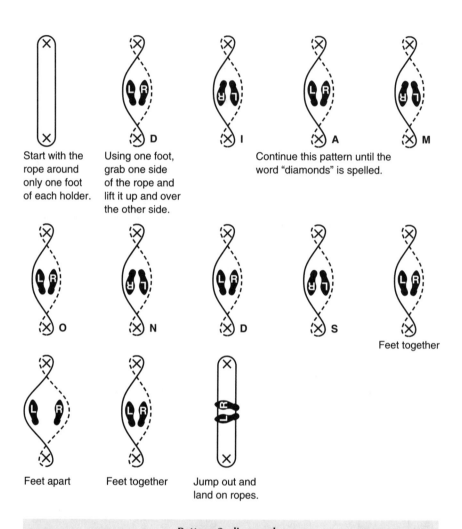

Start with the rope around only one foot of each holder.

Using one foot, grab one side of the rope and lift it up and over the other side. **D**

I

Continue this pattern until the word "diamonds" is spelled.

A

M

O

N

D

S

Feet together

Feet apart

Feet together

Jump out and land on ropes.

Pattern 2: diamonds.

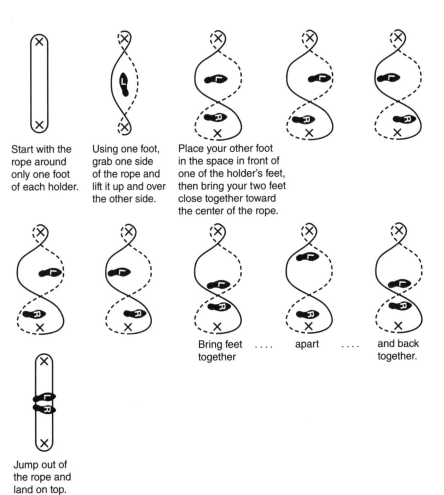

Start with the rope around only one foot of each holder.

Using one foot, grab one side of the rope and lift it up and over the other side.

Place your other foot in the space in front of one of the holder's feet, then bring your two feet close together toward the center of the rope.

Bring feet together .... apart .... and back together.

Jump out of the rope and land on top.

Pattern 3: sailboats.

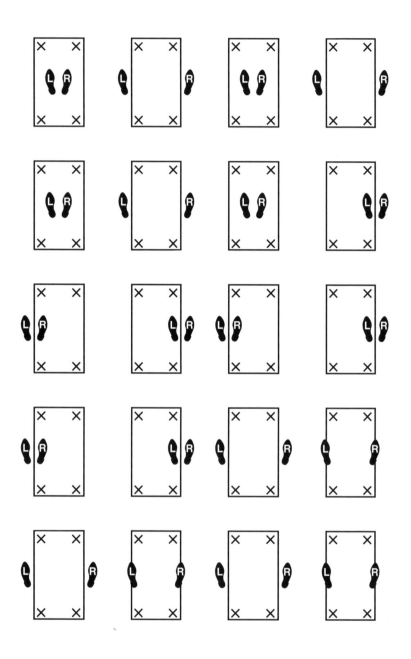

Pattern 4: Chinese.

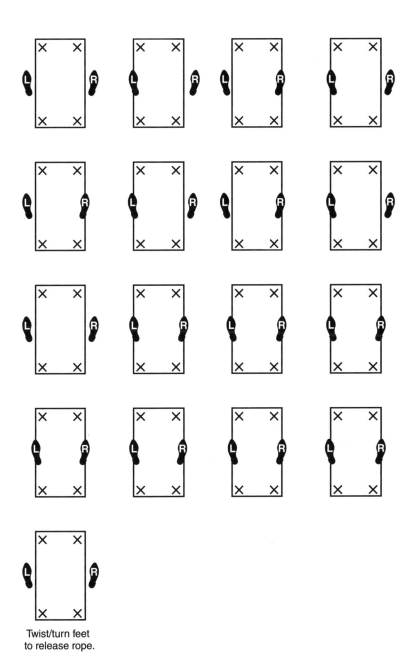

Twist/turn feet
to release rope.

Pattern 4: Chinese (continued).

TINIKLING

Tinikling originated in the Leyte province located in the Visayas islands group of the Philippines. The name *Tinikling* comes from the tikling bird, which the Leyte people describe as unique and extremely agile. This bird was adept at maneuvering through tree branches and grass. The tikling bird ate the rice crops from the paddies, so the angry farmers set traps made of bamboo poles to stop them. However, the agile birds escaped the traps.

The game tinikling comes from the days when the Philippines were under Spanish rule and the people worked in the rice paddies as slaves. If the slaves were not working fast enough, the owners made them stand between two sticks covered with thorns. The owners banged the sticks together and struck the slaves on their ankles. The slaves attempted to escape the beatings by jumping away from the sticks.

EQUIPMENT NEEDED

For each group:

- 2 PVC (polyvinyl chloride) poles 6 feet (2 m) long and 1.5 inches (4 cm) in diameter
- 2 PVC poles 2.5 feet (approximately 1 m) long and 1.5 inches (4 cm) in diameter
- Map showing the Philippines

HOW TO MAKE EQUIPMENT

1. Make poles in the listed dimensions using PVC piping from a hardware store.
2. Cut two pieces of PVC pipe 3 feet (1 m) long and attach them together using a PVC coupler to make a pole 6 feet (2 m) long. Repeat this step to make the required number of 6 foot (2 m) poles.
3. Cut 2.5 foot (1 m) long pieces of PVC and keep separately. Remember you will need two of these poles for each set.
4. Attach an end cap to the other end of the PVC pipe. Attach an end cap to both sides of the 2.5 foot (1 m) pieces.
5. You may wish to color the end caps of each set of poles with a different color. This will make it easier to keep track of equipment and keep players in groups.

HOW TO PLAY

1. Players divide into groups of at least 3 people. Two players will bang the sticks while the others jump.

2. Various diagrams can be posted explaining each set of steps (see figure). Each line represents a stick, the letter L represents the left foot, and the letter R represents the right foot.

3. After they have completed the set diagrams, players may create their own dances incorporating the steps they've learned.

SAFETY

Beginning players often accidentally strike the jumping player in the ankles with the poles. Players can reduce the risk of this accident by practicing the rhythm without poles. Follow these steps:

1. Players begin the practice without poles. On a set count, players should strike both hands on the floor twice and then clap their hands twice. The rhythm should be even and steady: *BANG...BANG....CLAP.... CLAP...repeat.*

2. When players have mastered this exercise, they can practice with a partner using the poles.

3. When players have mastered the rhythm with the poles, they may return to normal play.

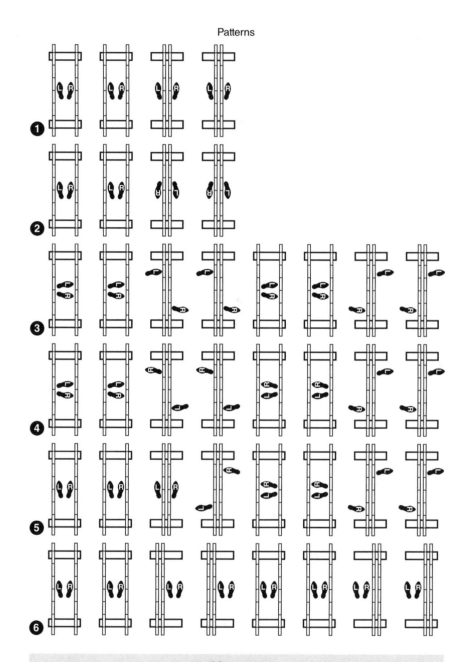

Tinikling pattern.

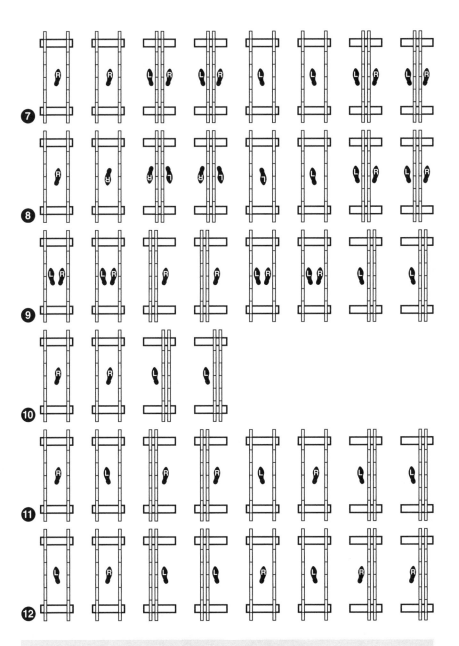

Tinikling pattern (continued).

DOUBLE DUTCH

Double Dutch can be traced back to the time of the ancient Phoenician, Egyptian, and Chinese cultures. Rope makers plied their craft with one end of a strand of hemp tied around their waists and the other attached to a wheel. They worked cooperatively with each other as they walked backward and twisted the rope uniformly. The workers that collected the hemp for the spinners were called *runners*. The runners had to jump over the moving ropes to complete their deliveries quickly. These workers may have created a leisure activity based on their work. In the game, the spinners became the *rope turners* and the runners became the *jumpers*. Double Dutch is a rope-skipping exercise that is played with 2 ropes turned in opposite directions like an eggbeater. A third person jumps inside the turning ropes.

Dutch immigrants in the portion of North America that is now New York brought the game with them. As the children played the game, they recited poems and sang songs in their native language. English settlers who came to the area later could not understand the songs and took to calling the game *double Dutch*.

In the 1940s and 1950s, jumping rope became popular in New York City because it was safe and affordable. Young girls were able to play near their homes where their mothers could see them. They used laundry clotheslines for rope. Double Dutch fell out of favor in the late 1950s when more families bought televisions. In 1973, two New York City police officers resurrected the game as a healthy alternative to the destructive behaviors many girls face in the city. They called the program *Rope Not Dope*.

EQUIPMENT NEEDED

For each group:

■ 2 ropes 12 to 16 feet (4 to 5 m) long or
■ 1 rope 24 to 32 feet (7 to 10 m) long

HOW TO PLAY

There are several different aspects to double Dutch: rope turning, jumping from a cold start, how to enter and exit when the ropes are turning, and patterns for entering and exiting.

Rope Turning

1. The two players who will be turning the rope stand facing each other and hold the rope down at their sides. They should decide which rope will begin the rotation.

2. Players move the hand holding the first rope out to the side and up to begin its rotation.

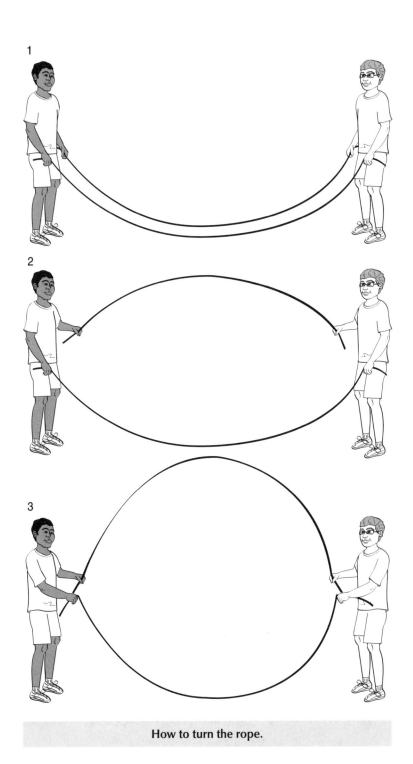

How to turn the rope.

3. When the first rope is about to reach the halfway point of its rotation (directly overhead), players turn the second rope in the same manner but in the opposite direction.

4. Players continue this process, creating a pattern with the ropes that looks like the motion of an eggbeater.

Tips for Rope Turning

▪ Players should keep a little tension on the ropes to maintain control.

▪ They should make sure the ropes hit the floor with each rotation.

▪ They should keep a steady beat.

▪ Players should try to make the shape of a circle with the ropes.

BEGINNERS MAY WISH TO USE TWO ROPES OF DIFFERENT COLORS SO THEY CAN SEE THE MOVEMENT MORE CLEARLY.

Beginning to Jump From a Cold Start

1. The jumper stands in between the two ropes.

2. When each rope reaches the floor, the jumper hops over it. This process continues for each revolution of the ropes.

Tips for Jumping

▪ Players should jump with both feet and land on the balls of their feet.

▪ They should hop approximately 2 inches (5 cm) off the ground.

▪ Players should only hop once for each rotation of the rope.

Entering the Ropes to Begin Jumping

1. While the ropes are already turning, the jumper stands next to one of the turners and watches the rope on the far side.

2. The turner calls out, "ready" the first time that rope passes the jumper's face, "set" the second time, and "go" the third time. The jumper enters when the turner says, "go."

3. The jumper takes one long step, lands on both feet in the middle of the ropes, and keeps jumping with single bounces.

Exiting the Ropes After Jumping

1. While jumping, the jumper moves closer to the exit end and watches the rope in the turner's hand on the opposite side.

2. On each turn of the opposite rope, the jumper calls "ready," "set," and "go," and exits on "go" by jumping over the rope toward the exit.

3. The jumper lands on both feet and steps away from the turner.

Jumping from a cold start.

Tips for Entering and Exiting

▪ Jumpers should feel extremely comfortable with a cold start.

▪ They should listen and watch the rhythm of the ropes before entering.

▪ Players can mark a spot on the floor for the center point of the ropes.

▪ Jumpers should watch the far rope and ignore the close one.

▪ Turners should move the rope slowly until the jumper is comfortable.

Patterns for Entering and Exiting in a Group Setting

▪ Jumpers form a line next to one of the turners.

▪ The first jumper will enter the ropes in the manner previously described.

▪ When finished, the jumper will exit the ropes on the end opposite to the starting point.

▪ The next jumper will enter the ropes in the same manner. While that person is jumping, the first jumper forms a new line at the opposite end.

▪ When all players have jumped and have moved over to the new line, the cycle repeats from the other end.

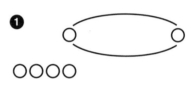

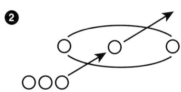

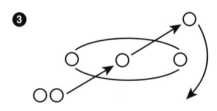

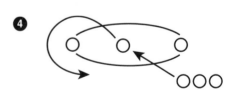

Entering and exiting as a group.

INTERNATIONAL SPORTS AND GAMES

UNIT 5

1. Chinese jump rope is said to be a combination of two games. What are they?

2. Why did double Dutch fall out of popular favor?

3. Name one of the origins of tinikling.

4. Name at least two skills that double Dutch, Chinese jump rope, and tinikling share.

5. Are there any similarities between all three games?

MATCH THE GAME WITH THE COUNTRY

• •

_____ Tinikling   A. China

_____ Double Dutch   B. Philippines

_____ Chinese jump rope   C. Colonial United States

From G. Horowitz, 2009, *International Games: Building Skills Through Multicultural Play* (Champaign, IL: Human Kinetics).

TEAM
SPORTS

SKYROS

The Greek game of skyros is a fast-moving version of the American game of ultimate Frisbee that uses a ball in place of a disk. Skyros players use passing skills similar to basketball to move the ball down the field to score a goal. Scoring a goal in skyros is similar to scoring a touchdown in American football. Any player who catches the ball in the goal area scores a point for the team. The major difference is that once skyros players have possession of the ball, they can no longer run.

EQUIPMENT NEEDED

- ▪ Map showing Greece
- ▪ Pinnies (vests worn to identify team members)
- ▪ Playground ball, volleyball, or foam soccer ball
- ▪ Gymnasium or outdoor playing field

HOW TO PLAY

1. Players divide into two teams of equal number.
2. The playing area is marked with a midline and two end lines an equal distance away on either side. If players are using a gymnasium, the half-court line can serve as the midline, and the walls can serve as the boundaries. If players are outside, they may mark the field.
3. Teams line up on opposite end lines.
4. The ball is placed on the midline. When the whistle blows, players from both teams rush to get the ball.

5. The object of the game is for a team to move the ball down the field and pass it to a teammate standing behind the opposite baseline. Players on the opposing team try to intercept the ball and score points by reaching the other baseline.

6. Skyros is not a contact sport, so players may not touch each other to gain possession of the ball.

7. Players may only pass and catch the ball. Players holding the ball cannot run. In order to continue to move the ball, they must pass it to another player. This passing technique is similar to basketball.

8. The game never stops. After a team scores a goal, possession of the ball goes to the other team. Play continues until the designated end, which can be defined by either a set number of points or the end of a timed session.

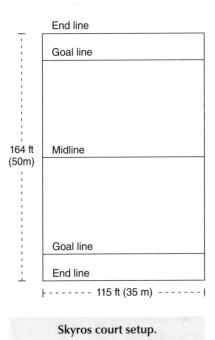

Skyros court setup.

BUROINJIN

Buroinjin is a game from the Kabi Kabi people of Southeastern Queensland in Australia. The game gets its name from the ball, which is made from kangaroo skin, stuffed with grass, and sewed together with tendons. Buroinjin is similar to skyros, but the player with the ball is allowed to run until tagged. After being tagged, the player has 3 seconds to pass the ball. Possession changes sides in one of two ways; the other team may intercept the ball or gain possession if they tag the team controlling the ball four times. Buroinjin is a popular game in schools today because of its easy rules and minimal equipment.

EQUIPMENT NEEDED

- ▦ Map showing Australia
- ▦ Pinnies
- ▦ Playground ball, volleyball, or foam ball

HOW TO PLAY

1. Players divide into two teams of equal number.
2. The playing area is marked with a midline and two end lines an equal distance away on either side. If players are using a gymnasium, the half-court line can serve as the midline, and the walls can serve as the boundaries. If players are outside, they may mark an outdoor field.
3. Each team lines up on opposite end lines.
4. The ball is placed on the midline. When the whistle blows, players from both teams rush to get the ball.
5. The object of the game is for a team to move the ball down the field and pass it to a teammate standing behind the opposite baseline. Players on the opposing team try to intercept the ball and score points by reaching the other baseline.

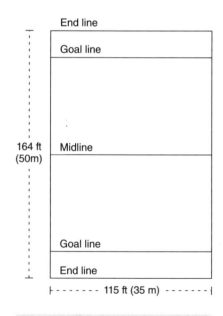

Buroinjin court setup.

6. Players may run with the ball until they are tagged. After being tagged, a player may take two steps, but then must pass the ball. If tagged while standing still, the player has 3 seconds to pass the ball.

7. Possession of the ball changes after each score or after a team has been tagged a total of four times. The number of tags may be raised to six for younger or beginning players.

8. Play continues until the designated end, which can be defined by either a set number of points or the end of a timed session.

TEAM HANDBALL

In 1919, at the Berlin Physical Education School, Professor Carl Schelenz combined the Danish game of haandbold, the Czechoslovakian game of hazena, and the German game of torball to create team handball. Team handball is a sport that features passing skills similar to basketball. Players move the ball down the court using bounce, chest, or overhead passes. They score points by throwing the ball into a small goal area at the end of the court.

Team handball quickly grew in popularity. In 1928, the International Amateur Handball Federation was formed. Team handball was featured in the Olympic Games as a demonstration sport in 1928 and 1932, and became a fully-recognized Olympic sport in 1936.

EQUIPMENT NEEDED

■ Map showing Germany

■ Small foam or playground-style balls of various sizes. The size of the ball depends on the age of the players, but it must fit in the players' palms.

■ 2 portable soccer nets

■ Cones to mark off playing field

HOW TO PLAY

1. The field is marked off with the cones. The field dimensions can vary based on the number and age of players. Use a basketball court as a gauge or half a regulation soccer field. If playing indoors, players may use an area slightly larger than a basketball court.

2. Players divide into teams of equal number. The game is traditionally played outdoors with teams of 11 players and indoors with teams of 7 players. The size of the teams may be altered based on the age of the players and the space available.

3. The game begins with a coin toss to determine who starts the game. The winner takes the ball and begins play with a throw-off (similar to inbounding the ball in basketball).

4. The object of the game is for teams to throw the ball into their own goal area. Teams score a point for each goal.

5. The length of the game is determined by the age and experience of the players and by the space allotted for play.

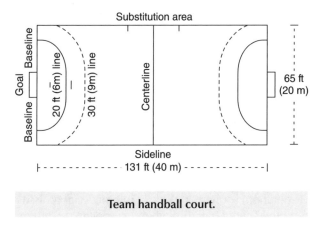

Team handball court.

Rules

- The ball may be dribbled (bounced on the floor or ground) for an unlimited amount of time.
- Players may take as many as three steps holding the ball. After they take three steps, players must dribble the ball again.
- Players may hold the ball for up to three seconds.
- Players may not throw the ball at others.
- Players may not pull, hit, or punch the ball out of an opponent's hands. The defending team can try to gain possession of the ball by intercepting a pass.

TCHOUKBALL

In the 1960s, Swiss biologist Dr. Hermann Brandt invented tchoukball while researching the frequency of injuries players sustain during physical activity. Dr. Brandt looked for the elements necessary for a team sport with a low risk of injury. The game gets its name from the "tchouk" sound the ball makes when it rebounds off the frame. A tchoukball frame is basically an angled miniature trampoline.

Tchoukball was first played in the 1970s. The game developed slowly, finally gaining notice in the 1980s when it became the 3rd most popular sport in Taiwan. Switzerland and England founded the FITB (International Tchoukball Federation) soon after to foster international growth of the sport. Italy also promoted Tchoukball through the European growth movement.

EQUIPMENT NEEDED

▪ Map showing Switzerland

▪ Small foam or playground-style ball. The size of the ball may vary with the age of the players but it must fit in the palm of the hand.

▪ 2 miniature trampolines. Players can contact the International Tchoukball Federation for names of businesses that sell these trampolines.

▪ Cones to mark off playing field

OBJECT OF THE GAME

Players throw the ball at the miniature trampoline or another rebounding surface so that it bounces off the rebounding surface and moves toward the floor quickly. The team on defense tries to catch the ball before it hits the floor. The team on offense tries to throw the ball in a manner that sends it to the floor as quickly as possible and prevents the defensive team from catching it. If the defending team is unsuccessful in catching the ball, the offensive team scores a point.

HOW TO PLAY

1. Cones are used to mark off a playing area approximately the size of a small soccer field.

2. Players divide into teams of equal number. The game is traditionally played with teams of 9, but team size can be altered based on the age of the players and the amount of space available.

3. Players toss a coin to determine who starts the game. The winner of the coin toss takes the ball and begins play with a throw-off (similar to inbounding the ball in basketball).

4. The length of the game is determined by the age and experience of the players and by the space allotted for play.

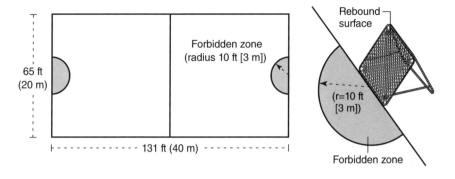

Tchoukball court and tchoukball frame.

RULES

■ Teams may attempt to score at either of the two rebounding surfaces located at opposite ends of the playing area.

■ Players may not intercept the ball or interfere with the player in possession of the ball.

■ Teams may pass the ball three times among players per possession. After three passes, a member of the team must attempt to score.

■ Any player receiving a pass may take as many as three steps. Players may not travel with the ball at any time.

■ Players are not allowed to enter the area within a 10-foot (3-m) radius of the rebounding surfaces that is called the *forbidden zone*.

■ If a pass is incomplete, the other team gains possession of the ball.

The defensive team can score a point if one of the following scenarios occurs:

■ The offensive team fails to strike the rebounding surface when the shooter throws the ball.

■ The ball lands out of bounds after striking the rebounding surface.

■ The ball bounces off the rebounding surface and strikes the shooter.

■ The ball lands in the forbidden zone either before or after the shot.

VARIATION OF PLAY

Players form teams of 9 and determine the number of points for the winning tally. When a team reaches that score, the losing team returns to the sidelines and a new team takes its place. The teams that are waiting to play assist continuity of play by standing along the sidelines and throwing stray balls back inbounds.

RUGBY

Rugby began in 10th-century England as a team game in which players kicked and threw an inflated pig bladder. Neighboring villages played against each other and traveled many miles between towns for matches. These games had very few rules.

In the late 17th century, a more structured form of rugby became popular in English schools. One rule was that players could not run with the ball. There is a legend that a student at Rugby school named Webb Ellis added some excitement to the game by running with the ball. The legend may not be true, but debates were held for 40 years in Britain on the issue of running in rugby.

Rugby students took the game with them to the universities and formed rugby clubs. The first one was at Cambridge University. In 1845, loose rules were established but not all the clubs knew the rules or followed them. In 1870, 22 clubs met and formed the Rugby Football Unit. In 1871, official rules were adopted.

EQUIPMENT NEEDED

- 1 rugby ball or 1 American football
- 4 cones to mark off the playing field
- 2 sets of belts with removable flags

HOW TO PLAY

1. Players divide into two teams of equal number.
2. Each player receives a flag belt.
3. Players toss a coin to determine the first player. The winner of the coin toss begins the game with a free toss, which is a two-handed pass to a teammate made on the referee's signal.
4. Play continues according to the rules for as long as time will allow or until a set amount of points have been earned.

RULES

- A *try* is worth one point, and occurs when a player crosses the goal line with the ball and presses it down on the ground. Younger children may score a point by merely crossing the line for greater ease and safety.
- Players may pass backward or to the side but may never throw the ball forward.
- In this version of rugby, players make a *tackle* by removing a flag from the ball carrier's belt. The ball carrier cannot fend off the opponents, spin around, or shield the flags, but may outrun or dodge the opponents. The defender returns the ribbon after the attacker has passed the ball.

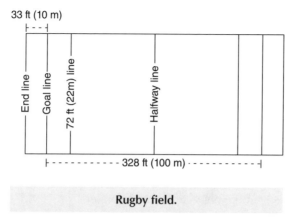

Rugby field.

- A free pass is also used to restart a game. The player in possession of the ball makes a two-handed pass to a teammate on the referee's signal. The opposing team may only begin to move after the pass is completed.
- If either the ball or the ball carrier goes out of bounds, the other team receives a free pass from the sideline where the ball went out.

ADVANCED RULES

- A *knock-on* occurs when a player attempts to catch the ball, fumbles it, and knocks it to the ground in the direction of the goal.
- When a tag, or tackle, is made, all defenders must move back to their side of the ball. An *offside* penalty may occur for a number of reasons during a tag: the defenders may intentionally stand on the offense's side of the ball, block the pass, or wait for an interception. When an offside penalty occurs, the attackers get a free pass.
- The *advantage* rule is used to keep the game moving with as few stoppages as possible. If a penalty occurs, play is not immediately halted. The referee waits to see whether either team gains a territorial or strategic advantage. If the penalty does not benefit the offending team, play should be allowed to continue. If the offending team does gain an advantage, the referee stops play and awards a free pass to the other team at the site of the original infraction.
- Beginners should play without a set number of tags. As the level of play advances, the offensive team may receive a set number of tags. When the team has been tagged that number of times, they must attempt to score a try. If they are unsuccessful, a *turnover* occurs. The defensive team is awarded a free pass at the spot of the last tag and play resumes.

CRICKET

Some people believe that the origin of cricket is connected to the Northern Indian and Pakistani bat-and-ball games. They think that these games moved from India to Persia and then to Europe. The game of cricket combines throwing and fielding skills from ancient Greece and a bat from South Asia. The bat called a *danda* comes from India. When the two elements are combined, they form an early version of the cricket game we know today.

Like many other recreational pursuits, cricket was banned in the 14th and 15th centuries by military officials who believed that the game distracted soldiers from their exercises. By the 16th century, cricket was once again legal and became more popular and widespread.

EQUIPMENT NEEDED

For skill-building exercises:

■ 1 Wiffle ball for each pair of players
■ Construction paper

For games:

■ 2 wickets
■ 2 flat bats
■ 2 bases (any rubber ground marker can be used)

BASIC SKILL BUILDING

1. Construction paper (9 inches by 14 inches) is fastened to the wall at approximately the height of a wicket.
2. A line is marked 30 feet (9 m) from the wall.
3. Players practice throwing the Wiffle ball at the target from a distance of 10 feet (3 m). After the players become successful from this distance, they should take a few steps back and begin again. Players continue in this manner until they are able to throw accurately from the 30 foot (9 m) line.
4. Once all players are comfortable with throwing and aiming, they move on to the full game.

How to Play

THESE ARE MODIFIED RULES, AND DIFFER FROM OFFICIAL CRICKET TO ENSURE MAXIMUM PARTICIPATION AND MAKE IT EASIER FOR ALL TO UNDERSTAND.

1. Players divide into two teams of equal number.
2. The field is set up with the 2 wickets in the middle of the field 30 feet (9 m) apart from each other. The wickets may be placed closer to each other for younger players or beginners.
3. Place the bail on the wicket so it is balanced on all three uprights.

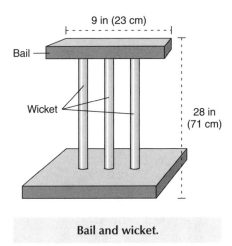

Bail and wicket.

4. One base sits 30 inches (76 cm) in front of each wicket.
5. The pitcher's goal is to throw the ball toward the opposite wicket in an attempt to knock the bail off. The batter's goal is to protect the bail and wicket by hitting the ball into the field.
6. The batter stands next to the base in a way that does not block the wicket.

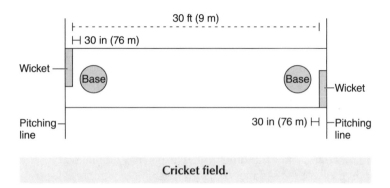

Cricket field.

Rules

- Batters must stand with the bat touching the base while waiting for the pitch.
- Pitchers may not cross the imaginary line that is even with the wicket and extends across the field. This line may be marked on the field ahead of time.
- Fielders stand spread around the entire field without specific positions.

Scoring

- One run is scored each time the batters reach the opposite base safely. They must touch the base with the bat rather than a foot.
- Batters may attempt to steal a base when the ball is released. Both batters must run to the opposite bases at the same time.
- Runs count only if both runners have reached their bases before the bail is knocked off.

Registering Outs

A team may score an out in the following ways:

- The pitcher successfully knocks the bail off the wicket with the pitch.
- The batter is not touching the base with the bat when the pitcher releases the ball.
- A player catches the ball after the batter hits it and before it hits the ground.
- A fielder knocks the bail off the wicket with the ball before the batter reaches the base.

■ A batter knocks the bail off the wicket with the bat or a body part.

■ The batter blocks the fielder from fielding the ball.

IN THE MODIFIED GAME, PLAYERS MAY DECIDE HOW TO END AN INNING. THEY CAN SET A NUMBER OF OUTS PER SIDE OR A MAXIMUM NUMBER OF RUNS BEFORE SIDES MUST CHANGE.

Name _____

INTERNATIONAL SPORTS AND GAMES

UNIT 6

1. Where does the game of tchoukball get its name?

2. What game played in the United States is similar to the game of skyros?

3. What game played in the United States would you consider to be a relative of cricket?

4. Is there any sport in the United States that compares to rugby?

5. What sport in this unit is the most similar to soccer?

MATCH THE GAME WITH THE COUNTRY

_____ Skyros   A. Australia

_____ Tchoukball   B. Germany

_____ Buroinjin   C. England

_____ Cricket   D. Greece

_____ Rugby   E. Pakistan

_____ Team handball   F. Switzerland

From G. Horowitz, 2009, *International Games: Building Skills Through Multicultural Play* (Champaign, IL: Human Kinetics).

STRENGTH

Tᴜɢ-ᴏꜰ-Wᴀʀ

The sport of tug-of-war can be traced back approximately 4000 years through the records of many civilizations and countries. Artwork found in an ancient Egyptian tomb illustrates a ropeless tug-of-war match. In ancient Greece, tug-of-war was both a competitive sport and a training exercise. The Scandinavian Vikings used animal skins instead of rope and competed by pulling the skins over a fire in preparation for war. The Chinese trained for tug-of-war competitions using one main rope with many side ropes. Tug-of-war spread through Asia in the 13th and 14th centuries as competitions became more popular.

Originally, tug-of-war was used to settle disputes between neighboring villages. Each of the villages made a straw rope of certain specifications and brought it to a predetermined site. The villagers then tied the two ropes together. One end of this new rope was designated as *male* and the other was *female*. The villagers stood behind their end of the rope, took a firm hold, and prepared to pull. Each village's goal was to pull the midline of the rope past a designated line on the ground and toward their side. They hoped that the *female* side would win because it was symbolic of a good future harvest.

Modern-day tug-of-war may have come from colonial Britain's sailors. The men controlled the ships by pulling on ropes attached to the steering mechanism. During calm moments at sea, the sailors played rope-pulling games on deck to keep fit and to engage in friendly competition. The British army took the game to India, where it spread quickly.

Eᴏᴜɪᴘᴍᴇɴᴛ Nᴇᴇᴅᴇᴅ

- ■ Map showing Egypt, Greece, China, India, England, and Scandinavia
- ■ 4 large cones
- ■ 4 track-and-field batons

- 4 belts with removable flags
- 1 roll of duct tape
- 4-way tug-of-war rope

GAME SETUP

- The playing area is set up as shown in the diagram.
- The flag football belts are threaded around the batons and tightened.
- The batons are placed on top of the cones and secured with duct tape.
- The flags are attached to the batons with Velcro.
- The 4 cones are placed on the field equally distant from the center and approximately 3 to 4 arm's lengths apart.

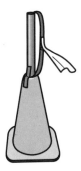

Placement of batons on cones.

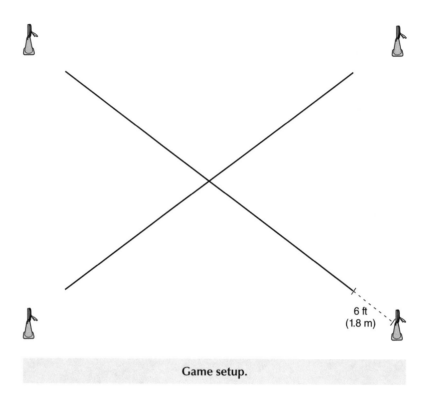

Game setup.

HOW TO PLAY

1. Players divide into four teams of equal number. If the group is co-ed, the teams should have an equal number of boys and girls on each side.

2. Players line up behind their team's side of the rope and find a place to hold on.

3. Hold the center part of the rope, ensure that all players have a firm grip, then signal the beginning of the match by blowing a whistle and dropping the rope.

4. Each team pulls backward on the rope in their respective directions. Each team is trying to move closer to the cone in order to pull the flag off.

5. The match is completed when one team pulls the flag from the cone.

NO MEMBER OF THE TEAM MAY RELEASE THE ROPE FOR ANY LENGTH OF TIME TO OBTAIN THE FLAG.

HIGHLAND GAMES

Heavy throwing events are a common form of recreation in Celtic countries, and can be traced back to 1829 BC. The Irish *Book of Leinster* details competitions held in Taillten, or modern-day Telltown, from 1829 BC to 554 BC. The games were then resurrected in the early 10th century and sustained until 1166 AD. Strength games are also featured in Scotland's Highland Games.

The Scottish chiefs of the Highland territories held contests to find strong warriors to defend their territories from British invasion. These contests may have been the basis of the Highland Games. Today's Highland Games feature strength contests like the stone throw, weight throws, hammer throw, caber toss, and sheaf toss (an event in which competitors throw a bale of hay with a pitchfork). In this book, we cover the following games: caber toss, Braemar stone put, hammer toss, weight toss for height, and weight toss for distance.

SAFETY FOR THROWING EVENTS

- Players should compete on a field or open space where those who are not throwing can wait out of the way. All other players should maintain a minimum distance of 10 feet (3 m) from the thrower.
- Players should not retrieve a thrown item until the throwing is over and the area is clear.

Caber Toss

The caber toss, in which players throw a large wooden pole end over end, is the most recognizable of Highland Game strength events. Records of the caber toss date back to the 16th century. The game's origin is unknown but it may have begun in the 16th century when people used large poles to break through barriers. Others believe that the game began when people moved logs to create a path over fast-moving mountain streams.

Equipment Needed

- Map showing Scotland
- 1 homemade caber 10 feet long and 4 inches in diameter
- 5 cones

Building a Caber

1. Take a PVC pipe that is 4 inches (10 cm) in diameter and 10 feet (3 m) in length, glue a PVC cap to one end, and secure the area with duct tape. Repeat this process for the desired number of cabers.
2. Fill each PVC pipe with varying amounts of sand or soil to create cabers with a range of weight.
3. Glue the other end cap in place and secure the area with duct tape.

Consult with a hardware store employee to find a glue that is strong enough to hold the caber together. Check the weight limit of the glue and avoid overfilling the caber with sand.

How to Play

1. The throwing area is set up with 2 cones on the ground 3 feet (1 m) apart. A line is drawn between the cones. Players stand four steps behind the line.
2. Players pick up the cabers and hold them in front of their bodies at the base. The ends of the cabers should rest on their shoulders.
3. The throwers jog forward and release the caber, tossing it so it will travel end over end, before they cross the line.
4. The throwers' goal is to make the caber land on the original lower end, stand upright, and fall perfectly forward. This position is called 12 o'clock and is a perfect score. Scoring is based on accuracy rather than distance.

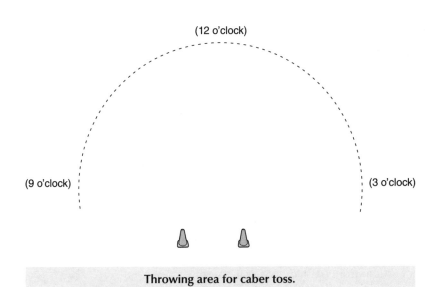

(12 o'clock)

(9 o'clock)

(3 o'clock)

Throwing area for caber toss.

BRAEMAR STONE PUT

The stone put is one of the oldest Scottish strength contests. The event is named for the town of Braemar where soldiers trained during the winter months. In the stone put, competitors pushed a weight over a distance. The Braemar stone put is an earlier version of the modern shot put.

EQUIPMENT NEEDED

- Map showing Scotland
- Shot puts varying in size from 6 to 16 pounds (3 to 7 kg)
- Floor tape or a piece of wood 4 to 6 feet (1 to 2 m) long for indoor shots
- Line markers for outdoor shots

HOW TO PLAY

1. Throwers stand perpendicular to the line known as a *trig* with their legs shoulder-width apart. They place the nondominant foot either against the trig or touching the line.
2. Throwers lean so that the body weight is on the dominant leg.
3. They place the stone or shot against the neck and support it with the dominant arm.
4. Throwers turn toward the trig, pushing off with their legs.
5. When they near their starting position, they push the shot forward and slightly upward. The motion is similar to when people put their hands out in front of them to signal a stop.
6. Throwers continue to push through the throw by continuing the motion until their arms are straight.

HAMMER TOSS

The Scottish hammer toss is the ancestor of the Olympic hammer throw. The original game piece was a sledge hammer that men threw as far as possible to show their strength.

EQUIPMENT NEEDED

▪ Map showing Scotland

▪ Track-and-field hammers of various weights or homemade hammers (see instructions for making hammers in the following section)

▪ Floor tape or a piece of wood 4 to 6 feet (1 to 2 m) long for indoor play

▪ Line markers for outdoor play

BUILDING A HAMMER

1. Take a PVC pipe 1 inch (2.5 cm) in diameter and 3 feet (1 m) in length, glue a PVC cap to one end, and secure the area with duct tape. Repeat this process for the desired number of hammers.

2. Fill each PVC pipe with varying amounts of sand or soil to create hammers with a range of weights.

3. Glue the other end cap in place and secure the area with duct tape.

CONSULT WITH A HARDWARE STORE EMPLOYEE TO FIND A GLUE THAT IS STRONG ENOUGH TO HOLD THE HAMMER TOGETHER. CHECK THE WEIGHT LIMIT OF THE GLUE AND AVOID OVERFILLING THE HAMMER WITH SAND.

HOW TO PLAY

1. Players stand with their backs to the field.

2. They use a golf-like grip to hold the hammer on the dominant side of the body.

3. Moving from front to back, players swing the hammer around their heads while keeping their knees slightly bent. Right-handed throwers should swing right to left and left-handed throwers should swing left to right.

4. As the player swings the hammer, it will begin to develop a high point and a low point. The low point should be directly in front of the player and the high point should be directly behind the player's head. At the high point, the hammer will be aimed at the field, which is ultimately the direction of the throw.

5. Players complete a few revolutions of the hammer swing, then release the hammer when they are comfortable. They should execute the release right before the hammer reaches the front of the throwing field.

6. Players should straighten their legs as they release the hammer.

7. They should follow through, or continue the rotating motion of the arm, after they release the hammer.

8. The winner of the hammer throw is the player who throws the hammer the farthest.

WEIGHT TOSS FOR HEIGHT

The weight toss for height is also known as weight over the bar. The object of the game is to throw an object approximately 56 pounds (25 kg) over a bar using one hand. Like other heavy events, ancient societies used the weight toss for height to discover their strongest members.

EQUIPMENT NEEDED

■ Map showing Scotland

■ Medicine balls of varying weights with handles

■ PVC pipe

■ PVC couplers (two L-shaped couplers for each crossbar)

BUILDING A CROSSBAR

1. Cut three pieces of PVC pipe to lengths of 5 to 6 feet (1.5 to 2 m).
2. Attach L-shaped couplers to one end of each of the pipes.
3. Use the third piece to connect the pipes together.

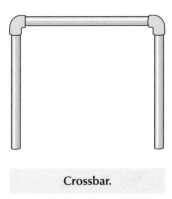

Crossbar.

HOW TO PLAY

1. Two players hold the crossbar straight (refer to the preceding drawing) by the handles.
2. The throwers stand facing the bar with their legs shoulder-width apart.
3. They grasp the ball with one hand and swing it back and forth between their legs until they generate enough force to toss the ball over the crossbar.

4. After each successful toss, the players holding the crossbar raise it a set amount.

5. If the ball touches the bar, it is not considered successful. Only clean tosses count.

SAFETY

The crossbar should be long enough so that the players holding the bar are at a safe distance from the thrower and the ball.

WEIGHT TOSS FOR DISTANCE

In ancient Scotland, boys had to be able to throw a stone a certain distance to be considered a man. This is a possible origin of the weight toss for distance. A weight was attached to a short chain and thrown with one hand using a spinning motion.

EQUIPMENT NEEDED

- Map showing Scotland
- Medicine balls of varying weights with handles
- Cones

HOW TO PLAY

1. Throwers stand at the rear of the throwing area facing the field. Their feet should be shoulder-width apart.
2. They hold the weight with the dominant hand.
3. Throwers slowly swing the weight back and forth on the dominant side of the body.
4. To throw, they step forward with the dominant foot and swing the weight forward.
5. When the dominant foot lands, the throwers bring the opposite foot around to the front, beginning a spin.
6. When the throwers complete this revolution, they bring the dominant foot back around so that they face the field, and they release the weight. This motion is similar to that of the modern discus throw.
7. The winner of the weight toss for distance is the player who throws the weight the farthest.

SAFETY

- Players may practice throwing the weight without the spin.
- Players may practice the spin without the weight.
- Players who are not throwing should stand behind the throwing area.

Name _____

INTERNATIONAL SPORTS AND GAMES

1. What country played tug-of-war using one main rope with multiple side ropes?

2. What two Highland Game events gave rise to two modern-day Olympic events?

3. What did the chiefs of the Highland territories use the heavy events for?

MATCH THE GAME WITH THE EQUIPMENT
• •

_____ Tug-of-war   A. Shots

_____ Caber toss   B. Hay bale

_____ Braemar stone put   C. Weighted pipes 3 feet (1 m) long

_____ Hammer throw   D. Medicine balls with handles

_____ Weight toss for height   E. Weighted pipes 10 feet (3 m) long

_____ Sheaf toss   F. Rope

From G. Horowitz, 2009, *International Games: Building Skills Through Multicultural Play* (Champaign, IL: Human Kinetics).

BIBLIOGRAPHY

Badminton history. *Perimeter Badminton Club.* 2003. Perimeter Church of Duluth, Georgia. 13 December 2005. http://perimeterbadminton.com/History.htm.

Baldwin, Pete. The history of kubb. *Kubb: The Viking game.* PlayKubb UK. 3 January 2006. www.kubb.co.uk/history.htm.

Barbarash, Barbara. *Multicultural games.* Champaign, IL: Human Kinetics, 1997.

Broglio, Ron. History of bocce. *Collegium ad buxeas.* 2003. Collegium Ad Buxeas. 21 November 2005. www.bocce.org/history.html.

Calegari, Julio. About tchoukball. *A brief summary of tchoukball.* 2004. International Tchoukball Federation (FITB). 7 January 2006. www.tagb.org.uk/tchoukball/summary.htm.

Chan, Patrick. History and development: A game of yesterday, today and the future. *Bay Area Sepak Tawrak.* 2004. AOL.com. 21 November 2005. http://members.aol.com/sftakraw/history.html.

Chinese jump rope. *Wikipedia.* 2005. Wikipedia. 24 December 2005. http://en.wikipedia.org/wiki/Chinese_jump_rope.

Double Dutch, fun and great exercise. *African American history.* 2005. African American Registry. 24 December 2005. www.aaregistry.com/african_american_history/1966/Double_Dutch_fun_and_great_exercise.

Drummer, Gail. Team handball. *Disability sports—Team handball.* 2002. Michigan State University. 13 January 2006. http://edweb6.educ.msu.edu/kin866/Sports/spteamhandball.htm.

Falconer, Aaron. Kubb—The game a thousand years in the making. *Kubb.com.* 2003. New Zealand Kubb. 31 December 2005. http://nzkubb.co.nz.

Football in old Korea. *Society & the arts.* 2002. Korea Now: Biweekly Magazine. 13 December 2005. http://kn.koreaherald.co.kr/SITE/data/html_dir/2002/06/21/200206210006.asp.

Game handball. *ClearLead Inc Sports.* ClearLead, Inc. 13 December 2005. www.clearleadinc.com/site/game-handball.html.

Guerra, Jenica. Ancient Hawaiian sports. *Ancient Hawaiian Sports.* 1998. University of Hawaii System. 7 January 2006. www2.hawaii.edu/~jenica/portfolio/HIsports.html.

Haggett, Rex. Hand shuttlecock. *Shuttlecock games of the world.* Compuserve Our World. 21 November 2005. http://ourworld.compuserve.com/homepages/Rexhaggett.

Henkel, Steven. Tinikling ideas. *Bethel.edu.* 2002. Bethel University. 22 December 2005. www.bethel.edu/~shenkel/PhysicalActivities/Rhythms/Tinikling/TinikleIdeas.html.

Hickok, Ralph. Sports history: Bocce. *HickokSports.com.* 2001. Hickok sports: Everything you wanted to know about sports. 31 December 2005. www.hickoksports.com/history/bocce.shtml.

History of cricket. *Wikipedia.* 2006. Wikipedia. 17 February 2006. http://en.wikipedia.org/wiki/History_of_cricket.

History of double Dutch. *Girl Scouts: Where girls grow strong.* Girl Scouts. 16 December 2005. http://home1.gte.net/info/double_dutch.htm.

The history of double Dutch. *National Double Dutch League.* 2003. National Double Dutch League. 16 December 2005. www.nationaldoubledutchleague.com/History.htm.

History of footbag. *Hacky Sack info.* Footbags.com. 23 December 2005. www.x-village.com/ Web%20Sites/Footbags.com%20Pages/fbinfo.html.

History of rugby. *SportsKnowHow.com—History of rugby.* 2004. SportsKnowHow.com. 20 December 2005. www.sportsknowhow.com/rugby/history/rugby-history.shtml.

Indigenous traditional games. *Australian government—Australian sports commission.* 2000. Australian Sports Commission. 20 January 2006. www.ausport.gov.au/__data/assets/pdf_ file/0008/123587/adult_games.pdf.

Khan, Tehmosp. History of cricket: 700 AD-1700 AD. *The earliest cricket.* 2006. Seattle Cricket Club. 20 February 2006. www.seattlecricket.com/history/earliest.htm.

Lankford, Mary. *Hopscotch around the world.* New York: Morrow, 1992.

Leonard, Nick. Tag rugby—The rules for tag rugby. *Coaching rugby.* 2001. Coaching Rugby.com. 12 March 2006. www.coachingrugby.com/tag/laws/laws.htm.

Masters, James. The online guide to traditional games: Battledore and shuttlecock. *The online guide to traditional games.* 2005. Traditional Sports and Games. 17 December 2005. www. tradgames.org.uk/games/Battledore~Shuttlecock.htm.

Mockford, James. Undokai—Japanese games. *National clearinghouse for U.S.–Japanese studies.* Indiana University. 16 December 2005. www.indiana.edu/~japan/LP/LS27.html.

Petanque. *Wikipedia.* 2005. Wikipedia. 3 January 2006. http://en.wikipedia.org/wiki/ Petanque.

Philippine national dance--Tinikling! *National Pilipino folk ensemble.* 2005. National Pilipino Folk Ensemble. 2 May 2005. www.likha.org/galleries/tinikling.asp.

Rene, Ray. The sport of team handball. *USA team handball.* 2005. United States Olympic Committee. 27 November 2005. www.usateamhandball.org/sport.html.

Salley, David. Hopscotch by Dagonell the juggler. *Dagonell's home page.* Canisius College. 22 December 2005. www-cs.canisius.edu/~salley/Articles/hopscotch.html.

Seagrist, Ryan. History of bowling. *Essortment: Information and advice you want to know.* 2002. Pagewise. 4 February 2006. www.essortment.com/historyofbowli_rkdx.htm.

Sullivan, David. History of horseshoe pitching. *HorseshoePitching.com.* 2005. National Horse-shoe Pitchers Association of America. 20 December 2005. www.horseshoepitching.com/ gameinfo/history.shtml.

Szendy, Szilvia. Children's folklore: Hungarian hopscotch. *Children's folklore, a universal anthology written by children and for children of the world.* 2005. Geocities. 23 December 2005. www. geocities.com/childrenfolklore/games_hungary.html?200523.

Team handball. *Team handball history & team handball rules.* 2005. Johann & Sandra's Web. 13 January 2006. www.johann-sandra.com/handball.htm.

Traditional children's games: Hopscotch. *Traditional children's games played around the world: Hopscotch.* Topics Online Magazine. 22 December 2005. www.topics-mag.com/edition11/ games-hopscotch.htm.

Traditional sports—other. *Traditional sports.* 2005. 13 December 2005. Korea.com: Gateway to Korea. www.korea.net/korea/kor_loca.asp?code=J010204.

Trueman, Nigel. Origins of rugby. *Rugby football history—Origins of rugby.* 2004. Rugby Football History. 20 December 2005. www.rugbyfootballhistory.com/originsofrugby.htm.

Whiteman, Susan. Hopscotch: A history. *Hopscotch history and variation.* 2005. Albany University. 22 December 2005. www.albany.edu/~sw7656/.

Zoomgames: Turn off your computer and play. *Zoom activities.* 1998. PBS Kids. 31 December 2005. http://pbskids.org/zoom/activities/games/ulumiaka.html.

ABOUT THE AUTHOR

Gayle L. Horowitz is a health and physical education teacher of students in grades 6 to 12 in Flushing, New York. A teacher for 14 years, she has worked with a program called Students with Interrupted Formal Education. This program helps at-risk immigrant students, many of whom become excited about education when they see a game from their native land.

In her spare time, Ms. Horowitz enjoys going on long walks with her partner and playing with her twin boys. She also holds a black belt in judo and was the New York State women's heavyweight judo champion in 2004.

You'll find other outstanding
physical activity resources at
www.HumanKinetics.com